JEFFERSONIAN DEMOCRACY
IN
NEW ENGLAND

By
WILLIAM A. ROBINSON

This Essay Won the John Addison Porter Prize
Yale University, 1913

AMS PRESS
NEW YORK

Reprinted from the edition of 1916, New Haven
First AMS EDITION published 1969
Manufactured in the United States of America

Library of Congress Catalog Card Number: 70-100523
SBN: 404-00632-9

AMS PRESS, INC.
New York, N.Y. 10003

PREFACE

Although New England history since 1789 has for the most part received much less study than the Colonial and Revolutionary periods, one topic, Federalism, has received exceptional attention. The opposition, however, has been neglected. The New England branch of Thomas Jefferson's party had certain disadvantages. Its opponent was the party of wealth and culture whose members wrote the great controversial papers, delivered the memorable orations, and edited the ablest newspapers and pamphlets of the day. It had few leaders of outstanding ability and personality to interest the biographer. Furthermore the bitter partisanship of the age has in some cases passed into subsequent histories and biographies, with advantage to the Federalists. Nevertheless, the New England Republicans performed important services, both local and national, in a period full of domestic and foreign difficulties. The following study was begun at the suggestion of Professor Allen Johnson and carried on under his direction while the author was a student in the Graduate School of Yale University. In its original essay form it was awarded in 1913 the John Addison Porter prize, established by the Kingsley Trust Association (Scroll and Key Society of Yale College). It has subsequently been revised and enlarged. The author takes this opportunity to express his deep appreciation of Professor Johnson's interest and assistance at all stages of the work. Material for the study has been found in various New England libraries. The authorities of the American Antiquarian Society, the Massachusetts Historical Society, the Massachusetts State Library, the Boston Athenæum, and the Yale University Library have given valuable assistance which is gratefully acknowledged.

CONTENTS

LIST OF ILLUSTRATIONS

CHAPTER I

POLITICAL CONDITIONS IN NEW ENGLAND, 1789-1797

By the adoption of a national constitution and the inauguration of the new government in 1789 the scope of political activity in the United States was infinitely enlarged. Party history, in the modern sense, dates from this time. But in the earlier stages, party development is hard to trace. There is, as in Homer's description of a battle, a great deal about the words and actions of the leaders and little about the rank and file. This, however, is due to existing conditions and it took several years for leaders to build up and organize their followers into great parties extending throughout the Union. The men who met in the first two Congresses to transact the business of the new nation were divided into opposing factions at a very early date;[1] their constituents followed their example. In some cases party divisions already existed and were continued under new names; in others, divisions occurred during Washington's administrations.

New England was a region where national parties were slow to develop. There had been in the past party divisions extending throughout the region. The quarrels with the mother country during the colonial era had

---

[1] Fisher Ames described the members of the House as containing, among other types, a body of "violent republicans, as they think fit to style themselves, who are new lights in politics, who would make not the law but the people king," etc. Ames to Minot, July 8, 1789. Works of Fisher Ames, I, 62.

divided people into the Whigs and Tories of the Revolution, but the result of the war was the elimination of the minority party. Its most influential members went to Canada, those who were left, at first sullen and resentful, gradually became reconciled to independence and republican government. The Revolutionary War created the same disturbances that have followed our other wars. There was the usual distress caused by destruction of life and property, the usual difficulty in meeting payment of debts, the usual amount of speculation.

The appearance of the paper money parties was due to the hard times which began soon after the restoration of peace, and New England suffered as severely as any part of the country from the activity of these factions. In Massachusetts the Shays Rebellion marked the culmination of this movement, while in Rhode Island its strength was sufficient to keep the state out of the Union until 1790. The adoption of the Federal Constitution was a great victory for the advocates of honest money and efficient government. Their opponents in most cases accepted the result and supported the new government without question.

For several years following 1789, New England politics seem to have been devoid of excitement. There was little inducement to form parties in local matters. The town meeting handled a great deal of the public business most closely touching affairs of the ordinary citizen. The state governments had but a narrow range of activity and the number of state officials was small. An examination of New England legislative enactments for this period shows few matters involving principles on which parties might form; indeed, until 1810, most of the divisions recorded in the journals of the New England legislatures are on resolutions pertaining to national affairs.[2] A New York newspaper records as an example of the weighty business transacted by the Connecticut legislature, that the greater part of a session was once devoted to a debate on the advisability of laying a tax on dogs, and a subsequent legislature devoted almost as much time to debating its removal.[3]

There is little or no trace of party in the election of the state governors. In Massachusetts there was a long-continued struggle between the supporters of James Bowdoin and John Hancock, which gives a more modern aspect to the politics of that state.[4] There were political divisions in the other states, to be sure, but these were usually of a temporary character, as, for example, that in Vermont, which in 1789 interrupted for a year Thomas Chittenden's tenure of the governorship.[5] Once the disorders of the Confederation were over, the long terms of the governors are a political characteristic of New England.[6]

Interest in voting was not great. Property qualifications existed in all the states except Vermont, but only a small proportion of those qualified availed themselves

[2] AUSTIN, Life of Elbridge Gerry, II, 322. "The limited legislation of the states gives rise to few questions of high character. The general policy of all parties is in most respects the same in time of peace."

[3] Republican Watch Tower. Quoted by American Mercury, January 29, 1801. William Plumer, in a letter to Jeremiah Smith, January 4, 1793, discussing the last session of the New Hampshire legislature, writes that "much time has been spent to compel people to have their sleds and sleys of a particular width; but the bills were eventually lost." MSS., I, 215.

[4] A detailed study of these factions is given by A. E. Morse in The Federalist Party in Massachusetts to the Year 1800.

[5] THOMPSON, Civil History of Vermont, 86.

[6] Some of the more notable examples of long tenure of office in this period are, Thomas Chittenden, Vermont, 1777-1796, with the exception of the year 1789-1790; Arthur Fenner, Rhode Island, 1790-1804; John T. Gilman, New Hampshire, 1794-1805, 1813-1816; Caleb Strong, Massachusetts, 1800-1807, 1812-1816; Jonathan Trumbull, Connecticut, 1798-1809.

of the privilege.[7] This was especially true of Connecticut. State officers were voted on at the close of town meeting and large numbers left as soon as the local business was transacted.[8] In 1793 a newspaper writer complained that the chief magistrates were often chosen by one twentieth of the legal voters, and because of this lack of interest "the tools and connections of those who seek for office are left to execute their designs unmolested." The result was that a few families who had assumed leadership during the Revolution—not out of sympathy for the cause, but for self-aggrandizement— had acquired an unrepublican ascendancy and were inclined to regard any opposition as "actual rebellion against the reigning powers."[9]

In New Hampshire, William Plumer noticed that in the course of his career the interest of the mass of the people in political matters had steadily grown, and that the number of voters had risen from the proportion of one vote to seventeen inhabitants in 1790, to one to eleven in 1800, and to one to six in 1816.[10] It was a New England boast that they had long been free from the electioneering disorders of Pennsylvania and the South.

---

[7] LUETSCHER, Early Political Machinery in the United States, 25.

[8] GREENE, Development of Religious Liberty in Connecticut, 401. Plumer comments on decision of the New Hampshire legislature to choose presidential electors at joint session, opposed by the "antis" as "a violation of liberty," "The law will create little uneasiness in the people for few of them attend the elections." According to Plumer at the last election 2500 votes made a choice for electors as compared with nearly 17,000 cast for governor. MSS., I, 428. Plumer to Smith, June 14, 1800.

[9] Am. Mercury, April 1, 1793. "Algernon Sydney." (This was the common signature of Gideon Granger.) Ibid., April 15, see a reply by "Hamden," in which reference is made to the "tyrants of this state." The following comment expresses the same idea: "To revive the (almost dormant) principles of the Revolution and excite an universal attention to the duty of election is an undertaking which the immortal Sydney would not have been ashamed to acknowledge."

[10] PLUMER, Life of William Plumer, 432.

In national politics as well there is little evidence of party. In Massachusetts there were traces of Anti-federalist and Shays influence in some places and two Anti-federalists, Elbridge Gerry and Jonathan Grout, were chosen members of the first Congress. But party lines were not clearly drawn, as is shown by the large number of candidates presenting themselves and the difficulty, persisting for many years, in securing a majority for any one.[11] After 1800 party organization tended to do away with this difficulty.

In view of the probability that most of the men chosen to our first two Congresses were not party men, the subsequent affiliations of some of them may be of interest. New Hampshire included in her delegation John Langdon and Nicholas Gilman, both signers of the Federal Constitution and both Republicans at a later day. In Massachusetts the state senate was in control of the growing anti-Hancock faction, which had succeeded in securing the adoption of the Constitution in the face of strenuous opposition. They secured the election to the United States Senate of men afterwards famous as staunch Federalists.[12] Of the representatives chosen, Gerry was the only one of note who became a Republican. Rhode Island elected as her first representative the leader of the Anti-federalist faction, Benjamin Bourne,[13] who was later a Federalist. Her senators, Joseph Stanton and Theodore Foster, both became

---

11 MORSE, Fed. Party in Mass., 63, 67. Conditions in New Hampshire were similar. Plumer's comment on the approaching congressional election of 1790. MSS., I, 161. ''The people appear divided and trifles light as air unite and divide them.'' At the next election William Page writes to Plumer, June 26, 1792, ''All was confusion—the parties were not formed for electing members to Congress,'' etc., 211.

12 Ibid., 64.

13 F. G. BATES, Rhode Island and the Formation of the Union, 181.

Republicans. Connecticut was a state where Anti-federalism had been insignificant in extent[14] and the state naturally fell into control of men who sympathized heartily with the new Federalism of the Washington administration.[15] Vermont was admitted to the Union in 1791, and it is of special interest to note that the four men first sent to the national government were all prominent Republicans by 1796.[16] While an opposition party in Congress began at an early date, its membership was not constant and it was common for members to vote with both sides.

An address to the electors of Connecticut in 1790 shows clearly the absence of party principles in a congressional election. Representatives were chosen on a general ticket in this state. The voters are urged to keep in mind the fact that their congressmen will not merely represent the state, but act for the nation. They should choose the best speakers in the state, men of good character who are thirty-five or forty years of age. Two of them should have a good knowledge of commerce. Lastly—"avoid too much veneration for

[14] LIBBY, Geographical Distribution of the Vote of the Thirteen States on the Federal Constitution 1787-1788, 14.

[15] Between 1789 and 1815 only one member from Connecticut fell under suspicion of disaffection. This was Joshua Coit, elected in 1794. In the course of the difficulties with France he several times voted with the Republicans, stirring up great indignation in the state (Connecticut Courant, July 10, 1797). In 1798 he was defeated for renomination and died soon after (Courant, July 23, September 3, 1798). The following appears in the Columbian Centinel, September 15, 1798: "Coit by his vote once made himself the theme of Jacobin eulogy. . . . In the nomination list he was left far in the rear and it has pleased God now to remove him from the cares of this world."

[16] Most of the facts in regard to the New England members have been drawn from Appleton's Cyclopedia of American Biography.

Good short sketches of the Vermont members are given by J. G. ULLERY, Men of Vermont.

family names.'"[17] This document presents a striking contrast to the electioneering literature produced a few years later.

Party names are not much in evidence during these years. The supporters of the measures of the national government were in a majority of cases the same that had favored the adoption of the constitution in 1788, and they continued to call themselves Federalists. Their opponents styled themselves Republicans, though there was not any clear agreement as to what entitled a man to use this term. Thus, when the *Independent Chronicle* of Boston attempted to gloss over Clinton's sharp practices in the New York election of 1792 and styled him "a staunch Republican," the rival *Columbian Centinel* remarked: "The term has so often been applied in this paper to Anti-federalists, Insurgents, State Demagogues and professed enemies to the union of our common country, that it is difficult to ascertain its precise meaning.'"[18] In the previous year an address to the electors of the Bristol district of Massachusetts notes the fact that Phanuel Bishop (a former Anti-federalist) was making enemies by "his firmness in the cause of republicanism.'"[19] The use by the Federalists of the terms Jacobin and Democrat to denote their opponents becomes common in 1793, when interest in the French Revolution reached its height.

The enactments of the first two Congresses seem to

[17] Am. Mercury, September 6, 1790. For a similar address, United States Chronicle, August 2, 1792.

[18] July 28, 1798.

[19] U. S. Chronicle, July 14, 1791.

A writer in the Connecticut Courant, September 17, 1792, gives an account of a meeting with "one of Mr. Jefferson's disciples—who calls himself a true republican." He tells how decisively he defeated the "democratical Jeffersonian" in an argument relative to the position of the "well-born" in a republic.

have been received in New England with little opposition. New Hampshire for local reasons opposed the funding system and the assumption of state debts. There is some evidence of grumbling at the extravagance of Congress which had voted itself six dollars a day salary and was suspected of showing a desire to imitate the grandeur of Parliament.[20] The excise law which aroused such opposition in some quarters was received with indifference in New England, whose inhabitants had been used to similar taxation under state authority.[21]

The general tone of the New England press during these years is one of indifference to political agitations and in the occasional reviews of conditions throughout the Union, growing commerce and good business are emphasized as characteristic of the time, as contrasted with hard times and ill feeling in the past.[22] The outbreak of the war in Europe was expected to greatly benefit the American provision trade and to make American ships the chief carriers of the world's commerce.[23] But in 1792 the increasing acrimony of politics can be clearly seen, and complications growing out of the foreign situation soon became serious.

[20] Am. Mercury, September 21, October 19, 1789.

[21] Conn. Courant, December 31, 1792. It is interesting to note that the Chief Justice of the United States while on the Vermont circuit entered into an elaborate explanation and defense of the excise law, in an address to the grand jury at Bennington. See Col. Centinel, July 28, 1792. Some sympathy for the Whiskey Rebellion was expressed in Vermont. See Col. Centinel, September 15, 1794.

[22] See "political sketch of conditions throughout the country" quoted from U. S. Gazette by U. S. Chronicle, September 1, 8, 1791. The second of these articles has some excellent information on Massachusetts. Also, ibid., May 16, 1793; also Col. Centinel, May 16, 1792.

[23] U. S. Chronicle, March 7, 1793. Conn. Courant, December 8, 1792. "No matter what the issue of the French contest may be it will favor the United States. . . . Refugees will contribute to the prosperity of our country."

The re-election of the Vice-President in 1792 is generally regarded as the first great test of national party strength. In this New England showed decided unanimity and every electoral vote of the section was cast for John Adams. There is some scattered evidence that party feeling was increasing. "Political heresies are gaining ground among us," declares a writer in the *Columbian Centinel*, August 22, 1792. "Itinerant Jacobins" were said to be holding forth in the barrooms of Rhode Island and Vermont and endeavoring to stir up opposition.[24] But the activity of this year seems to be that of the politician, not of the people at large. "They have piped, but the people would not dance," declared the *Connecticut Courant*.[25] The vote for Adams was regarded with considerable satisfaction. The opposition had expected to gain support from Hancock in Massachusetts and Anti-federalist Rhode Island had been counted on. Vermont, whose representatives in Congress had shown radical tendencies, was also expected to vote against Adams, but her electors had been Federal.[26]

The effects of the foreign complications of 1793 on American politics have been too frequently stated to need any repetition. They were much the same in New England as in the rest of the country. The New Englanders were perhaps less given to sentimental enthu-

24 Am. Mercury, December 31, 1792. The paper gives some of the subjects of their lectures: "On the proper discipline of a file leader—how to make men follow their file leader." "The best method of recovering popularity—vote against all grants of money, vote against every grant of money."

25 December 31, 1792. As late as 1796 Plumer writes to Jeremiah Smith, August 12: "We are divided into two parties, Federalists and anti-federalists. . . . They [Langdon and others of the latter party] are taking infinite pains but the electors are too sensible to be duped by their artifices." MSS., I, 307.

26 Conn. Courant, February 11, 1793.

siasm than the people of other sections, but there was abundant sympathy for the French Revolution, and after 1793 equally vehement dislike. The Democratic societies made their appearance as elsewhere, but their chief seats of activity were Boston and western Vermont.[27] The formation of these societies introduced a new vigor into elections and the immediate effect was a marked increase in voting and general interest in public affairs. The measures necessitated by the administration's attempt to preserve neutrality furnished topics which were of interest to the citizens in every part of the Union. There was now no question as to the existence of real parties.

The political effect of the presence of a Democratic club was nowhere clearer than in Boston, and in 1794 there took place in this district the most exciting congressional contest that had yet occurred in New England—that between Fisher Ames and Dr. Charles Jarvis. A comparison of the candidates published in the *Independent Chronicle* is an interesting contrast to electioneering productions of earlier years. Ames was an advocate of measures extending the powers of the supreme executive magistrate; he was a panegyrist on British friendship; he had denounced a gallant nation now struggling for liberty; in the constitutional convention he had declared "democracy is a volcano." His opponent, Dr. Jarvis, had, during his career in the legislature, "made the rights of man his pole star." He had invariably supported Republican measures; he had opposed

---

[27] The best account of the Democratic clubs is in HAZEN, American Opinion of the French Revolution, 188-229.

See also LUETSCHER, Early Political Machinery, 32-62.

Spooner's Vermont Journal, November 18, 1796, has an account of the clubs of western Vermont. It mentions the fact that such organizations never appeared east of the Green Mountains.

consolidating the state governments by making them subject to the suits of individuals or to make Massachusetts subservient to monarchy by the purchase of stock in the national bank.[28] Ames won by a narrow margin.

A new political development at this time is apparent in the increased interest shown in the conduct of representatives, and there seems to be a new disposition to criticise votes in Congress as a matter of real interest to the constituent.[29] In the fall of 1794, twenty-three New England representatives signed a document explaining and defending their conduct during the previous session.[30]

The question of English relations was of course a phase of foreign policy and naturally emphasized the differences between the friends and opponents of a French alliance. The great feature of English relations was the Jay Treaty which became public in June, 1795, and almost at once a matter of controversy as intense as that following the Proclamation of Neutrality. Only two New England senators voted against its adoption, Langdon of New Hampshire and Robinson of Vermont, both becoming at once the theme of eulogy or abuse. Popular interest in the treaty was manifest in the number of resolutions passed in approval or condemnation. Bentley records that the Essex militia appeared at review with "Treaty" or "No Treaty" marked on their

[28] Independent Chronicle, October 27, 1794. The Boston papers of the day contain a great deal of electioneering material. See also MORSE, Fed. Party in Mass., 148. Works of Fisher Ames, 146-151, passim. LUETSCHER, Early Political Machinery, 59.

[29] Col. Centinel, April 30, 1794, contains an attack on Henry Dearborn for his support of measures which would ruin the commerce of the District of Maine.

[30] Col. Centinel, October 25, 1794. In the same issue mention is made that four New England representatives, Dearborn, J. S. Sherburne, Nicholas Gilman, and Wm. Lyman, had "enlisted under the banners of Southern representation."

knapsacks.[31] But the chief interest in the treaty is as a party test and since 1793 there had been a growing tendency to judge candidates by their attitude on national questions.[32] Party divisions were steadily becoming more clearly defined throughout New England.[33] In Massachusetts there was growing dissatisfaction with Governor Samuel Adams, who was a pronounced partisan of France.[34] In 1796 Adams announced that he would not be a candidate again and his popularity as a Revolutionary patriot no longer stood in the way of a fair party test. In Vermont the death of Thomas Chittenden, who had also been a barrier against party contests, had a similar effect. He had not been a party leader, while his successor, Isaac Tichenor, was a staunch Federalist.[35] Connecticut in 1794 and 1795 had gone through a fierce struggle over the disposal of the funds derived from the sale of western lands.[36] Public feeling was aroused and complaint begins to appear that the government was keeping the people in the dark and discouraging free inquiry by flattering disquisitions on steady habits.[37] Rhode Island and New Hampshire were as yet but slightly disturbed by parties.

In national politics the discussion of the last few

[31] Diary of William Bentley, II, 182. In reference to the election of 1796, ''Adams had rendered himself odious to the Federalists & was not in high esteem, from his age & character, with many of the Anti-Treaty party,'' 176.

[32] MORSE, Fed. Party in Mass., 140.

[33] BENTLEY, Diary, II, 174. March 12, 1796. ''Electioneering goes on in our own State & in New Hampshire. It extends itself in Boston for the petty Officers of the Town. This is the Commencement of a new Career.''

[34] MORSE, Fed. Party in Mass., 159.

[35] THOMPSON, Vermont, 84, 88.

[36] GREENE, Religious Liberty in Conn., 268-392.

[37] Am. Mercury, August 24, 1795.

years had made the issues clear and by 1796 the position
of New England is fairly well defined. All her electoral
votes were given to John Adams. In the Senate, John
Langdon was the only Republican. Langdon, in spite
of opposition due to his attitude toward the Jay Treaty,
had been re-elected in 1795, evidence that party lines
were not yet drawn in the New Hampshire legislature.[38] In the House, several active Republicans appeared after the elections of 1796. Samuel Dexter, one
of the ablest of the Massachusetts Federalists, had been
beaten by Joseph Varnum in 1795. Skinner appeared
from the Berkshire district. In western Vermont, "that
Nazareth of anti-federalism," Lyon had defeated a less
radical Republican, Israel Smith, and now opened his
boisterous congressional career. But the New England
representation in Congress was overwhelmingly Federalist. By the end of 1797 all the issues had been made
clear, the last New England state had chosen its position and Federalism had acquired an ascendancy that
took the opposition years of effort to destroy.

[38] MORISON, Life of Jeremiah Smith, 66. Smith, then a representative,
writes concerning Langdon's election: "If he is not elected he will I fear
be soured and rear up an anti-federal party in the state; set up democratic
clubs and poison the pure principles of our citizens. Let our people fall
into the hands of the devil but let them not fall into the hands of these
men."

CHAPTER II

THE GROWTH OF REPUBLICANISM, 1797-1800

The administration of John Adams closes the Federalist era of American politics. During his term the party recovered for a brief period the prestige it had lost during the years 1793-1796, only to go down in what proved to be final defeat in 1800. New England gave Adams all her electoral votes in 1796 and repeated the performance in 1800, but the vote of the latter year had no longer the same significance. New England Republicanism had been an uncertain quantity during Washington's administration, although it had begun to take more definite shape by 1796. The events of 1797 and 1798 checked its growth, and its adherents for a while appeared only as a factious and contemptible minority; by 1800 it had regained strength, and was formidable enough to threaten Federalist supremacy in four states.

Foreign affairs formed the chief interest of John Adams' administration. The course of events resulted in hostilities with France, and hostilities with France resulted in measures which tended to associate Federalism with extravagance, arbitrary government, and aristocratic tendencies. People were already divided on the question of French or British sympathy; the animosity between them was aggravated by the events of 1797-1798, and there follows that disgraceful era characterized by an utter lack of national spirit; when leaders abjectly apologized for the outrages of the European belligerents, and their followers drank toasts to Suvarov and Nelson, or held festivals in honor of French victories.[1] The satisfactory operation of the Jay Treaty and the depredations of France in 1797 led to a noticeable diminution of sympathy for that country. This was especially the case in New England, where losses were more severely felt. State elections were of little importance except in Massachusetts and Vermont, but in these states the strength of Federalism was decisively proved. In Massachusetts the candidates for the governorship were Increase Sumner, Federalist, and James Sullivan, Republican. The Federalist candidate was elected by a majority of 3752.[2] The fact that it was probably the first fair test of party strength gives a certain interest to the distribution of the vote. The Republican areas are fairly well defined; northern Berkshire, Middlesex, Norfolk and Bristol counties show strong Republican tendencies. In central Massachusetts, Federalism was predominant. In the District of Maine, York County and the region of the Kennebec show Republican strength.[3] In Vermont, parties were

---

[1] An interesting picture of public feeling at this time is given by Bentley. December 8, 1796. ''This evening our fire club annual supper. Men of quite opposite political views assemble & associate on the occasion. Says one, how finely Adet was drubbed in the Centinel. The french are deceitful. In another chair a whisper, Parson how some people curse the french such as you would not think of. I hope Jefferson will obtain the election & be president, I say nothing however. Says another, have you seen the new ed. of the Forresters, a new chapter gives the Jacobins the title of Mother Carey's chickens, etc. A good supper hushed all jealousies, & good wine cheered the heart. But unluckily brandy was served to some by mistake.'' Diary, II, 207. An item of later date shows a similar state of feeling. Spooner's Vermont Journal, January 15, 1810. ''The care of those nations, the defence of their claims, and apologies for their errors and crimes, seems to be the labor of too many of our writers.''

[2] MORSE, Fed. Party in Mass., 179.

[3] See map. Sullivan carried Middlesex, York, and Washington counties. Returns in Mass. Archives.

active.   Isaac Tichenor, a Federalist, was elected governor over Moses Robinson, who in the Senate had voted with Langdon against the ratification of the Jay Treaty, a victory which gave great satisfaction to the party throughout New England.[4]   Chipman, also a Federalist, was elected to the United States Senate.[5]

Congress, in response to the President's message, had taken steps towards placing the country in a state of defense.   Appropriations were made for harbor defense, the navy, and the army, and to meet increased expenditures new revenue measures were adopted.   Public opinion in New England was evidently in support of the government, for on June 27 George Cabot was able to write that, after a trip of four hundred miles through New England, one hundred and fifty miles of which had been on the Connecticut and Merrimac, he found people everywhere maintaining "more just sentiments."   This, he found, was especially true in New Hampshire and Vermont.   "I could not forbear to conclude," he writes, "that the disaffection in Boston and its vicinity is almost all that exists in New England for I consider the paltry opposition of Portsmouth as only sufficient to blow the fire of patriotism in the rest of the state of New Hampshire."[6]   The "paltry opposition of Portsmouth" was manifest in a special election of a congressman in November.   Woodbury Langdon carried the towns of Portsmouth and Rye, while his Federalist opponent, Peleg Sprague, received an almost unanimous vote in the interior towns.[7]

4 Col. Centinel, September 20, 1797.

5 Records of Governor and Council, IV, 142.

6 LODGE, Life and Letters of George Cabot, 140.   Cabot to O. Wolcott, June 27, 1797.

7 Oracle of the Day, November 4, 1797.

If events of 1797 had increased the power of the Federalist party, those of the succeeding year could not but have a similar effect. In April came the publication of the X. Y. Z. correspondence and the result was a flash of national spirit, a rare occurrence in this period. The opposition did not dare to stand out against the administration, which showed a determination to uphold national honor. Jefferson, always a shrewd observer, saw the change and wrote regretfully to Madison that the "popular movement" had been checked in the Eastern States.[8] His confidence that a closer view of war and taxes would again produce a change was fully justified by later events. Opposition was only silenced, it was still formidable.[9]

The state elections of this year seemed to indicate a rapid decline of Republicanism. In Connecticut there is evidence of more activity than usual. Both parties professed a horror of electioneering and endeavored to keep their manœuvres secret. The Federalists were reported to have held a caucus at Litchfield and to be actively engaged in gaining support for their candidates.[10] The Republicans, their opponents said, had gathered at Hartford on March 20, and conspired to introduce their fellows into the legislature and if possible secure the election to Congress of Mr. Granger and two other promising members of their party.[11] Whatever may be the truth of these reports, the old

8 FORD, Jefferson Writings, VII, 246.

9 Fisher Ames wrote to H. G. Otis on April 23, 1798: "The late communications have only smothered their rage; it is now a coal pit, lately it was an open fire." Works, I, 225. Again, to Timothy Pickering, June 4: "Not one Jacobin is changed, though many are dumb." Ibid., 227.

10 Am. Mercury, April 5, 1798.

11 Conn. Courant, April 2, 9, 1798.

state officers were returned and Connecticut Federalism remained unshaken.[12] Rhode Island re-elected most of her officers, including Governor Fenner, without much opposition.[13] New Hampshire and Massachusetts gave equally strong support to the Federalists.[14] In the latter state the Republicans showed a woeful decline in numbers. Fisher Ames had declared that the election of Increase Sumner would "kill faction" in the state, and for a time it seemed as though this hope would be realized.[15] The Vermont election was not held until October, and should, for local reasons, be considered by itself.

In the New England legislatures Federalism showed remarkable strength. The great party test was the address of confidence in the President. This was more than a perfunctory courtesy. At a time when there was such a lack of national feeling, to secure harmony between state and general governments was a matter of real significance. As a party test it showed the existence of a considerable body of representative citizens with common views on national questions. Until 1815 the attitude to be taken on national questions was always a matter of great interest when the legislature convened, and debate often raged over the wording of some

12 Noah Webster wrote to Pickering concerning this election: "There never was so full an election. The citizens of Connecticut have no wish to be involved in political disputes but have taken sides. The usual vote for governor and council has risen from 3000 to 7000. . . . The number of votes mustered by the clubs will not rise above 590." Pickering MSS., XXII, 156. Webster to Pickering, May 12, 1798.

13 Col. Centinel, May 9, 1798.

14 In New Hampshire out of 12,143 votes Gilman received 9397. Oracle of the Day, June 16, 1798.

In Massachusetts Sumner received 17,498, the votes in opposition (mostly for Sullivan) were 2167. Returns in Mass. Archives.

For comment on this election see MORSE, Fed. Party in Mass., 175.

15 Works, I, 186.

clause in reply to the governor's message in which reference was made to affairs at Washington.[16] In the course of the summer four of the New England legislatures passed resolutions declaring their confidence in the President. Vermont did likewise when the legislature met later in the year.[17] Massachusetts and Vermont both show a small, but evidently determined opposition, as it took no little courage to vote nay on such a measure. In the list of nays in Massachusetts appear the names of Henry Dearborn, Phanuel Bishop, Daniel Ilsley, and Ebenezer Seaver, all of whom sooner or later served in Congress as Republicans. Seven of the thirty votes in opposition were from Middlesex.[18]

In the congressional elections of this year the Republicans made but a poor showing, although there is more evidence of party voting than in 1796. In Connecticut, owing to the peculiar system in vogue whereby the voters nominated in one election and voted on those securing the highest vote at a second, the names of several suspected Jacobins appeared in the nomination list. The *Courant* raised the alarm. Connecticut must be

[16] In the Mass. House Journal, January 24, 1807, it is recorded that "after five hours' debate without an adjournment," the address to the President was adopted. XXVIII, 293, 294. Plumer in a letter to Jeremiah Smith, April 19, 1796, expresses the hope "that the Governor in his next communication will not dwell on matters relating to the General Government" because they are "apt to provoke disruptions." MSS., I, 294.

[17] Conn. Courant, July 16, gives the votes on these resolutions: Rhode Island, yeas, 60, nays, 0; Connecticut, yeas, 173, nays, 2; Massachusetts, yeas, 144, nays, 30; New Hampshire, yeas, 132, nays, 4.

In Vermont the vote stood 129-23. THOMPSON, Vermont, 88.

[18] House Journal, XIX, 54.

Dr. Nathaniel Ames on an undated page in his diary recorded the names of the thirty who voted in the negative, "names of the faithful minority in Gen'l Court June 7 on the question for addressing J. Adams, Pres. U. S. A. for committing us to the Lyon's paw." MSS. Diary of Nathaniel Ames, in possession of Dedham Historical Society. Nathaniel was a brother of the famous Fisher Ames, but a violent Republican.

spared the disgrace of electing to Congress any but the purest Federalists. The disorganizing sentiments of two men on the list were well known, those of a third were doubtful, and "he that doubteth in a spiritual sense is damned."[19] The people took the alarm, and as the same paper later recorded "to their everlasting honor, they not only shut out the new ones who aspired to office, but also purged the old nomination of the few democrats who had slyly crept into it. The nomination is now pure and of course the State runs no risk of being misrepresented in Congress for the next two years."[20] It was several years before Republicanism got fairly started in this state. Rhode Island, since her admission to the Union, had become Federalized. One of her representatives, Tillinghast, had voted with the "Gallatin junto" and was decisively beaten. His colleague, Champlin, was re-elected almost without opposition.[21]

Massachusetts elected only two Republicans. Varnum, who had taken a somewhat prominent part in the last session, won the Middlesex district and after four trials, Bishop carried Bristol. Even Berkshire, which had shown strong Republican tendencies, elected Theodore Sedgwick, a Federalist. The Boston district was carried by H. G. Otis over General William Heath, whom the *Centinel* with characteristic vehemence, described as a "ridiculous, despicable, weak minded, weak hearted Jacobin."[22] New Hampshire elected four Federalists on a general ticket by a very large majority.[23]

[19] April 2, 1798.

[20] September 3, 1798.

[21] Conn. Courant, August 27, September 3, 1798. Also Col. Centinel, September 15, state's vote—Tillinghast 2638, Brown 3992. "Such a man as Tillinghast was not re-elected in Rhode Island where the purest federalism pervades almost every town."

[22] November 3, 1798.

[23] Oracle of the Day, October 27, 1791. The lowest vote on the list was 446, the next highest 4637.

But the political situation in Vermont is perhaps the most interesting and significant in New England. The representative of her western district, Matthew Lyon, with his coarseness and aggressive democracy, had already drawn attention to himself and his constituents by his bout with Griswold.[24] The district was full of dissatisfaction and uneasiness. As early as January a convention had met at Wallingford, set up a liberty pole and protested against the stamp tax, actions which were similar to those in northeastern New York.[25] The state election in October, however, showed a decided majority for the Federalists. The legislature met, addressed the President and then proceeded to a wholesale removal of Republican officeholders. Among the "political deceases by Jacobin fever" were numbered three councillors, four county judges, one sheriff, four judges of probate, one attorney general, nineteen justices.[26] The

24 McLAUGHLIN, Matthew Lyon, 209-305.

25 Col. Centinel, January 20, 24, 1798. A letter in the latter number states that Lyon had franked to his constituents hundreds of copies of "that Pandora box of anarchy," the Philadelphia Aurora. "The poison operated on the minds of the unthinking" and was responsible for the Wallingford gathering. January 20, "A Bennington paper mentions that a spirit of insurgency similar to the above was rising in the back part of New York State!" See also Am. Mercury, January 25, 1798.

26 Ibid., December 8, 1798; also see October 31, November 7, 17, for this proscription. Also THOMPSON, Vermont, 89. The following extract from the Albany Centinel, quoted by Oracle of the Day, December 29, gives a good idea of the intolerant spirit of Federalism at this time: "Jacobinism is being punished in Vermont. Every Jacobin who held office under the government has been justly displaced. Judges, sheriffs, justices of the peace, have received the sentence 'Depart, ye cursed.' . . . A measure which should be universally imitated. . . . Consign the sons of clamor and sedition to neglect and contempt."

AMES, Diary, November 7: "The Devil reigns in Vermont; Judges and Justices all turned out of office for not returning back to Britain."

On June 20 the Centinel had recommended similar measures elsewhere. "Why does not the President tumble from their places the Collector, Loan Office Commissioner, and the Commander of the Revenue cutter at Ports-

number of removals at least shows that there was a considerable body of Republicans in the state.

The condition of state politics was not the only thing which served to draw the attention of New England, or in fact of the whole country, to Vermont. Matthew Lyon had already aroused the wrath of the Federalists, and the Sedition Act of July 14 offered a convenient weapon to use against him, especially as he was a candidate for re-election. In October he was convicted under this law and imprisoned at Vergennes.[27] The result of this prosecution was ominous for Federalism. In the indecisive September election Lyon had lacked a majority; at a second election, in December, while still in jail, he easily carried the district. More than fifteen hundred more votes were cast in the second election than in the first.[28] The conduct of the Federalists in this year must be remembered in view of the remarkable growth of the opposing party in the next two years.

Another matter which should be considered in connection with the events of 1798 was the reception of the Virginia and Kentucky resolutions in the New England legislatures. These documents voiced the protest of the opposition against the Alien and Sedition Laws and practically constituted a party manifesto against the administration. New England rejected them decisively. Rhode Island cast one vote in their favor; Connecticut, two; New Hampshire, none; Massachusetts, twenty-nine in the House, and one in the Senate. Of the twenty-nine, nineteen had voted against the address to John Adams in the preceding session.[29] The lone senator was

mouth? The ingrates ought not to eat the country's bread and betray her to France,'' etc. Plumer, in a letter to Secretary Wolcott, June 8, 1798, urges similar action against these officers. MSS., I, 397.

[27] McLaughlin, Lyon, 337-382.
[28] Ibid., 375.
[29] House Journal, XIX, 276.

John Bacon of Berkshire, elected to Congress two years later. These states considered the resolutions during the winter or spring sessions of 1799; the Vermont legislature did not meet until October, when the growth of the Republican party was seen in the fact that there were fifty votes on behalf of the Kentucky Resolutions, and fifty-two for the Virginia.[30]

Federalism attained its maximum power and popularity in 1798. The history of the next two years is of steadily growing opposition. The causes are not hard to find. The "popular movement," the check to which had been apparent to Jefferson, quickly revived when the first fervor of hostility to France had passed away. The conduct of the Federalists could not but irritate people who were beginning to take more interest in public affairs than ever before. The war taxes supplied the Republican orators with arguments which could be brought home to every farmer in New England. On the purely political side, the dissensions in the Federalist party undoubtedly weakened it; the Republican party was improving in organization and increasing its activity.

From 1796 on, there is expressed in Republican writings a growing hostility to "Aristocracy," including the clergy, the lawyers, merchants, and officeholders. The idea that the people were being kept in the dark finds frequent expression, and the overbearing attitude of the Federalists toward all opponents aggravated matters. In 1797 a writer in a New Hampshire paper complains that "anything opposed to the ideas of the Administration" constitutes "Jacobinism." "To be true Federalists, we must be at once deaf, dumb, and blind; we must hear nothing—say nothing—see noth-

30 F. M. ANDERSON, Contemporary Opinion of the Virginia and Kentucky Resolutions. Am. Hist. Rev., V, 58-63, 225 ff.

ing"—and the enactment of the Sedition Law in the following year seemed to indicate a determination to make citizens conform to this ideal.[31] The prosecutions under this law, the wholesale removals from office in Vermont, all seemed to indicate a determination to suppress political opposition as though it were treason. The people apparently were acquiescent, but even the Federalists did not believe this condition would last. Ames warned Pickering of the "folly of keeping the multitude long in suspense. . . . Keep them in action, and shift the scenes, and you may succeed."[32] The *Connecticut Courant* warned the state that although the Jacobins were silent, "This is ominous of evil. The murderer listens to see if all is quiet, then he begins. So it is with the Jacobins."[33] Republican opposition, however, was not expressed by the ballot until the following year. Liberty poles set up in various places were, however, indicative of the restless spirit pervading the people.[34] The

[31] Oracle of the Day, October 7, 1797. The following from the Ind. Chronicle, November 30, 1797, expresses the same ideas. "Sydney" on the basis of division of parties: "The Aristocrats are of the opinion that the people of this country are entirely incapable of supporting a government upon republican principles. . . . The Jacobins on the other hand, contend that a government formed upon an aggregation of Republics, beginning at the Town Meeting, widening into Counties and Districts and still further to a Governor, Council, and Legislature in each State and thereon the whole composing a Federal system which unites all in one common interest and the whole system supported by a frequent election of magistrates and rulers is most apt to preserve the political independence and to promote the happiness of the people." The hostility of the leading Federalists to popular government is well known.

[32] Works, I, 228.

[33] August 13, 1798.

[34] The inscription on the pole at Dedham is worth quoting. "No Stamp Act, No Sedition, no Alien Bills, no Land Tax, downfall to the Tyrants of America, peace and retirement to the President, long live the Vice President and the Minority, may moral virtue be the basis of civil government." Col. Centinel, November 13, 1798.

apparent supremacy of the Federalists was based on very insecure foundations.[35] The stamp tax, as has been mentioned, occasioned considerable stir in Vermont.[36] This, and the land tax, had the same result throughout New England. Jefferson's prophecy that "a nearer view of war and taxes" would affect public opinion was soon verified and early in 1799 he was able to note the discontent excited by the tax gatherer.[37] The dread of taxation which was characteristic of the age was used by the Republicans with great effect.[38] Money was scarce, the average amount of property small, and the New England farmer who had to make a living from the stony fields or among the stumps in Maine or Vermont lent ready ear to the stories of Federalist extravagance.[39] The land tax bogey had been brought out as one of the dangers of

[35] BENTLEY, Diary, II, 298. March 28, 1799. ''Our common topics are the captures of French vessels. Everything is done to excite our joy upon these events, but we rejoice with trembling. . . . Political violence in party is not a proof of quiet possession, and this stir makes us fear more from the directed strength than the progress of any party.''

[36] Conn. Courant, February 25, 1799. ''In none of the States has there been more clamor about the stamp law than in Vermont.''

[37] FORD, Jefferson Writings, VII, 313. Jefferson to Madison, January 3, 1799. An excellent illustration of the dislike for these measures is found in Nathaniel Ames' diary. January 23, 1799, ''Called on by Nehh Fales for dimensions of my house and windows and list of land for Direct tax of High Fed. tyrant Govert. Introduce it thus. Nat. Ames (regretting the short dawn of rational Liberty under the Confederation—deploring the blindness and apathy of that People who once dared to defy and trample on the minions of foreign tyrants, only to be trampled on by domestic traitors, in impudent junto, breaking the limits of the Sovreign—grated with the tyrant songs of 'Energy of Govert.—Tighten the reins of Govert.' only to stifle the chearing sound of the great sovreign's voice—forc'd to yield—instead of Law, to the mighty powers that be) exhibits this list and description of his house and land on the first day of October 1798.''

[38] See MORSE, Fed. Party in Mass., 177.

[39] LODGE, Cabot, 180. ''It is more grievous to observe the motives which govern the voters. They vote for the man who would vote against

the Jay Treaty.[40] The Federalist expenditures of 1798 were an admirable subject for denunciation and they were used unsparingly by the Republican papers during these two years.[41] The secrecy with which all political machinery was put in motion renders it difficult to judge as to how serious was the effort to secure control of the state governments. Most of our evidence comes from the Federalist press, but it seems probable that there was unusual activity among Republicans.[42] Election returns certainly show that the party was rapidly gaining ground. Jefferson, some years after, stated that a number of Republicans, seeing the complete control exercised by the Federalists in the national government, had retired to their respective states to organize and strengthen the opposition.[43] This was recognized at

taxes.'' See also Plumer MSS., I, 410, for Plumer's comment on opposition tactics in New Hampshire.

[40] Col. Centinel, September 26, 1795. ''How will the treaty engender a land tax? Because Virginians will not pay their debts? . . . The phantom has been exhibited at periods ever since 1789.''

[41] For interesting expressions of opinion on Taxes, see Ind. Chronicle, January 10, 14, 17, 21, 28, March 29, August 23, 1799. In Rhode Island the legislature passed resolutions recommending to the government of the United States a general property tax as a substitute for the land tax which was unduly burdensome to real estate. U. S. Chronicle, March 14, 1799. See Am. Mercury, March 22, 1798. A characteristic expression occurs. ''The most proper persons to appropriate money are those who know with what difficulty it is obtained.'' AMES, Diary, January 29, 1799. ''The great Sovereign Grumbles at unconstitutional tax.''

GIBBS, Memoirs of the Administrations of Washington and John Adams, II, 239. ''The Jacobins have lately become more systematical, I think, in their electioneering projects, and have in this part of the country availed themselves greatly of those momentary discontents which naturally follow the promulgation of a new tax. We are taking some pains, however, to keep the people steady, and, I hope, with a majority, these labors will succeed.'' Cabot to Wolcott, May 2, 1799.

[42] MORSE, Fed. Party in Mass., 176.

[43] JEFFERSON, Works, Wash. ed., IX, 507.

the time, and previous to the state election of 1799 the *Columbian Centinel* was warning the Federalists, that, finding it impossible to render the country subservient to France through the general government, they were now directing their force to effect it through the state governments, where, at least in the case of Massachusetts, an organized effort was being made to oust from the legislature "every man of honesty, independence, and federalism." A caucus at the close of the winter session of the General Court had set the "Jeffersonian puppets" at this task. "The correspondent of Mazzei is in the center of the circle. His myrmidons, faithful to their duty, act as he directs and bellow as he prescribes."[44] In Vermont, the exertions of "that fomenter of evil works, Matthew Lyon, and his cubs" were reported to be unusually active.[45] In the other states, politics seem to have been rather quiet until 1800, although in Connecticut the Stamford Democratic club, which, "as usual governed the elections in that town," was reported to be very active in stirring up excitement and discontent.[46]

In 1800 there was no longer any question about the determination of the Republicans to effect a revolution. The warnings of 1799 were repeated. In Connecticut the Republicans openly met at New Haven to organize their campaign and make nominations.[47] The

[44] April 6, 1799. *Ibid.*, April 17, May 1.

[45] *Ibid.*, October 5, 1799. Lyon about this time went to Kentucky "where," the Centinel remarked (October 30), "birds of a feather flock together." *Ibid.*, June 22. "The Vermont Lyon was at Knoxville, Tennessee the 29, April, after prowling over more than 1400 miles of territory. He speaks highly of the docility of his fellow brutes of Kentucky and Tennessee." Lyon had written of the prevalent Republicanism of the West.

[46] Conn. Courant, February 25, April 22, 1799.

[47] GREENE, Religious Liberty in Conn., 417. See also Conn. Courant, August 25, 1800, account of meeting on "Thermidor 20, reign of reason the 8th."

"private cabals" which had long existed were now replaced by an active campaign. "Rhetorical missionaries" were active, Aaron Burr adding his influence to that of Granger, Kirby, Edwards, and other local lights.[48] Burr, however, no mean judge of politics, was evidently not impressed with the progress of the party in this state, as he is reported to have remarked that "Connecticut must be given up. There is no hope for them. We may as soon attempt to revolutionize the kingdom of heaven."[49] The fact that the Republicans had drawn up a nomination for councillors seemed to the Federalists a proof of growing boldness and the *Courant* recorded that "for the first time they have had the audacity in the state of Connecticut to circulate printed tickets."[50] No attempt seems to have been made to run a candidate against Governor Trumbull, but efforts were directed against the council, the congressional delegation, and town representatives, the latter being especially important because choosing presidential electors.[51]

In Massachusetts a similar movement was in progress. So threatening was the situation that the legislative caucus which nominated Caleb Strong issued a special appeal to the electors, both the caucus and its address being a new feature in Massachusetts politics.[52] This document is an appeal for united action by the "friends of society, religion, and good order," in view of the growth of faction, and because "the enemies of our excellent Federal constitution are now striving to

---

[48] Conn. Courant, September 1, 8, 1800.

[49] *Ibid.*, April 27, 1801. This remark has also been attributed to other Republican leaders.

[50] September 1, 1800.

[51] *Ibid.*, August 18.

[52] LUETSCHER, Early Political Machinery, 121.

gain admittance into the administration of the individual state governments."[53]

New Hampshire had hitherto shown little evidence of party division, but in 1799 the inevitable break began. Almost thirty years later, when Jacksonian Democracy was struggling for a foothold in the state, Isaac Hill wrote to Henry Lee that "in 1798 with the exception of Langdon and a few sterling patriots, there could not be said to be in this state a party favorable to the principles of Thomas Jefferson."[54] The immediate cause of the new movement affords an example of the curious interworking of local and national affairs. The "paltry opposition" to Federalism in Portsmouth has been already noted. This "arch faction," so runs the Federalist history of the affair, were anxious to aid their friends in the South and to increase their own importance in the United States. Accordingly, led by John Langdon they organized a new bank, taking care to have subscribers to its stock scattered through the country districts. The bank made a business of making small loans on easy terms, apparently for the purpose of securing supporters for its managers. "The mischief spread like a pestilence" and when in 1799 the bank was refused a charter by the legislature and a law was passed restraining unincorporated institutions at the fall session there was great indignation. The only other bank then in the state—the New Hampshire Bank—

53 Col. Centinel, February 12, 1800. Bentley gives evidence as to the political activity of this year and also as to growth in popular influence in politics. Diary, II, 354, October 25, 1800. ''For the first time the zeal of Caucusing has been introduced into Salem. In former times particular men of influence have met to agree upon a candidate for office, but then the meeting was of few & all upon one side. Now parties are armed at all points & large associations are forming & alliances offensive & defensive as reputation, interest, & all men hold dear are involved in the controversies.''

54 Proceedings Mass. Hist. Soc., XLIII, 69.

was doing a flourishing business and the state owned a considerable interest in its stock. In any case, the attitude toward the Langdon bank was felt to be another piece of Federalist intolerance. Numerous Federalists had supported the petition of the new bank, and the result was that they joined with the Portsmouth faction in running for the governorship Judge Walker, nominally a Federalist, but described by Plumer to be of such contemptible character that "if his soul was drawn at full length on the point of a cambrick needle, to discover it would require the aid of the microscope."[55] A sharply contested campaign followed in the spring of 1800, an experience which the state had not yet undergone. Federalist opinion was unanimous in regarding the whole affair as a Jacobin ruse to start a division in the state.[56] Rhode Island and Vermont offer nothing of special interest during these years.

In short, in all New England the last two years of the century were characterized by a rapid increase in electioneering, and political interest on the part of the people was steadily growing.[57] The concrete evidence

[55] MSS., I, 108.

[56] This account is based largely on the "brief history of the rise and progress of the late electioneering manœuvres in New Hampshire," published in Col. Centinel, March 22, 1800. The Republicans in 1805 published a history of the matter as a campaign attack on Governor Gilman, making charges that he used the executive power to induce members to vote against incorporation. New Hampshire Gazette, February 26, March 5, 1805.

The legislative history of the bill is found in the House Journal for winter session 1799. See also PLUMER, Plumer, 138, 139. Also Plumer MSS., I, 408-425 passim.

The Col. Centinel, March 15, 1800, after discussing the activity of the Republicans who had abandoned Congress for the state legislatures, to "secure their pickets," remarks, "In New Hampshire a similar policy was practiced under cover of an ambuscade."

[57] In Massachusetts between 1798 and 1800 the vote for governor increased about 82 per cent.

in the form of election returns seems to verify Dr. Ames' view that there was "a general grumbling of the Great Sov'reign against its Agents attempting to veil, stupify, and then bleed it to fainting instead of helping to feed, arm and invigorate and enlighten it !!!"[58] That evidence, rather scanty unfortunately, must be considered. It shows a decided increase in Republican power in both state and national affairs.

The political activity which has been noted began to show results in 1799. Connecticut has no record of election returns but the press gives some evidence showing that the Republicans were making headway. When the Virginia and Kentucky Resolutions were under discussion it was reported that there were several "Jacobins" in the House but that they absented themselves when the vote was taken.[59] The elections were somewhat quiet in this year and the town of Stamford was reported to have cast about one third of the total Republican vote in the state.[60] The following year shows the actual increase in party strength. As a result of the summer's campaign, the *American Mercury*, now recognized as the organ of the new party for the state, recorded that there had been "an unexampled instance of the change of public opinion and the progress of Whig principles in this State. . . . In many towns where there was not a man who a few months ago avowed the cause of republicanism, the friends of liberty and the constitution have now a majority."[61] In 1799 the *Courant* had declared that in the legisla-

In New Hampshire the increase was 38 per cent. Vote in 1798, 12,143, Oracle of the Day, June 16. Vote in 1800, 16,762, Col. Centinel, June 14.
58 Diary, August 31, 1800.
59 Conn. Courant, June 3, 1799.
60 *Ibid.*, March 31, 1800.
61 September 26, 1800.

ture "democracy had not dared to show its hideous head,"[62] now in the spring session a bill for districting the state for congressional elections was boldly introduced,[63] and in the fall the Republicans mustered twenty-seven votes against a resolution appointing presidential electors.[64]

In Massachusetts the Republicans, with General William Heath as candidate—a man who could not be considered as a strong leader—polled over eight thousand votes in 1799, and elected about forty-five members to the General Court.[65] Heath carried Middlesex and Norfolk counties and received support in nearly every part of the state.[66] Fisher Ames was keenly aware of conditions and wrote in November that "on the whole, the rabies canina of Jacobinism has gradually spread, of late years, from the cities, where it was confined to docks and mob, to the country. I think it is still spreading silently, and why should it not?"[67]

Circumstances combined in 1800 to make elections close and exciting. The quarrel between John Adams and the faction of the party represented by Pickering undoubtedly weakened the Federalists.[68] The nomination of Gerry was also a shrewd move on the part of the Republicans, as he had both the prestige of long association with that party and his relations with John Adams were calculated to bring some Federalist votes.

62 June 3, 1799.
63 March 31, 1800.
64 October 27, 1800.
65 MORSE, Fed. Party in Mass., 176, 177.
66 Returns in Mass. Archives.
67 Works, I, 265. Ames to Gore, November 10, 1799. Cf. Plumer's remarks on the conduct of the Portsmouth "mobility." "The fashion does not take in the country—'tis confined to the compact part of that town." To Jeremiah Smith, October 17, 1795. MSS., I, 260.
68 MORSE, Fed. Party in Mass., 177.

It was admitted that he received considerable Federalist support.[69] The result of the election spread dismay among Federalists, as Gerry polled more than seventeen thousand votes, carrying six counties, including Suffolk and the capital.[70] The fact that Sumner had died in 1799 and the Federalist candidate, Caleb Strong, lacked his predecessor's popularity, must be taken into consideration in this result. But the Federalist majority, though reduced, was safe, and they had also a strong majority of votes in the General Court, which chose the presidential electors.

As a result of the campaign on the bank issue in New Hampshire there were over six thousand votes cast against Gilman, but as in Massachusetts, the legislature was safely Federalist and the "demon of Jacobinism was effectually laid for this year at least."[71] Vermont and Rhode Island also show Republican gains. In the former state, Tichenor, who had become very popular, was re-elected, but in the legislature the Federalist majority was reduced to thirty-four.[72] Two years earlier it had been over a hundred. Rhode Island had apparently little interest in state politics in 1799 and 1800. In the latter year there was a sharp contest for the lieutenant-governorship, no one, as in Connecticut, apparently having the temerity to contest the governor's position.[73] It is recorded in 1800, however, that Federalism was losing ground at an alarming rate,

69 Col. Centinel, April 16, 1800. *Ibid.*, October 1. The same complaint was made that Levi Lincoln was receiving Federalist votes in the fourth western district and that "many of the true faith were falling."

70 MORSE, Fed. Party in Mass., 179, 180.

71 Col. Centinel, June 14, 1800.

72 *Ibid.*, October 29.

73 Providence Journal, May 21, 1800.

owing to large desertions of men who had formerly been its supporters.[74]

The congressional elections show the same increase of Republicanism. Connecticut and New Hampshire, using general tickets, elected solid Federalist delegations, although in the former state three Republicans showed a considerable vote.[75] Rhode Island under the same system chose two Republicans, one of them being Tillinghast, beaten so decisively two years earlier—an indication of the impending revolution in that state.[76] Vermont maintained the same party balance, the eastern district electing a Federalist and the western a Republican. In Massachusetts the changes were marked. Bishop and Varnum were re-elected and the spread of Republicanism was seen in the election of John Bacon in Berkshire and Levi Lincoln in Worcester. Jacob Crowninshield, a Republican, was with difficulty beaten in southern Essex.[77] The election of Dr. William Eustis in the Boston district was also a severe blow to the Federalists.

The choice of presidential electors was perhaps the most important political event of the year. In all of the New England states except Rhode Island they were appointed by the legislature. In Massachusetts and Connecticut the decision to use this method provoked deep resentment among Republicans. In the former state it was adopted after a spirited debate by a vote of

[74] Col. Centinel, November 12, 1800.

[75] Conn. Courant, October 20, 1800. Hart 3250, Gilbert 2921, Granger 3012. The average vote for the Federalist ticket was 6773.

[76] Col. Centinel, September 27, 1800.

[77] An interesting item in connection with this latter district shows not only the issues of the day, but characteristic American shrewdness in discrediting an opponent. The Republicans circulated tickets bearing the English coat of arms over the Federalist's name, while that of their own candidate bore the American eagle. Col. Centinel, August 27, 1800. BENTLEY, Diary, II, 347.

122 to 71.[78] In Connecticut it was declared that the freemen had been "repeatedly and impudently robbed of one high privilege, choosing Electors," and "the right of suffrage is the citadel of liberty."[79] In Rhode Island, where "the good old cause ran greater risks than in any other state," the Federalist ticket won by the narrow majority of 193.[80]

But in summing up the political results of the year, Federalism is seen to be still firmly entrenched in New England. Four of the five governors were Federalist, Fenner of Rhode Island being nominally a non-partisan, though he had decided Republican sympathies. They controlled all the legislatures, they had elected all the United States senators, a very large majority of the representatives. Of the local institutions which contributed to the strength of the party, more will be said later. Clearly Republicanism was only beginning its conquest of New England.

[78] Col. Centinel, June 7, 1800. An abstract of the debate is given.

[79] Am. Mercury, September 20, 1800.

[80] *Ibid.*, December 6, 1800. The account states that "the eventual triumph of the Federal ticket was wholly owing to the unprecedented exertions of Providence." The vote stood, Federalist, 2343, Republican, 2150.

CHAPTER III

THE GROWTH OF REPUBLICANISM, 1800-1807

In 1800 Jefferson wrote to Granger of Connecticut discussing the principles of the Republican party and commenting on its remarkable growth throughout the country. He then remarked, "Still, should the whole body of New England continue in opposition to these principles of government, either knowingly or through delusion, our government will be a very uneasy one."[1] Two years later Fisher Ames was writing: "The federalists must entrench themselves in the State governments, and endeavor to make State justice and State power a shelter of the wise, and good, and rich, from the wild destroying rage of the Southern Jacobins. Such a post will be a high one, from which to combine in our favor the honest sentiments of New England at least. Public opinion must be addressed; must be purified from the dangerous errors with which it is infected; and, above all, must be roused from the prevailing apathy, the still more absurd and perilous trust in the moderation of the violent, and the tendency of revolution itself to liberty."[2] The political history of New England from 1800 to 1815 was the story of the contest of these opposing ideas.

As has been noted in discussing the elections of 1800, the Republicans had greater strength in Vermont and Rhode Island than elsewhere in New England. The

---

[1] FORD, Jefferson Writings, VII, 450.
[2] Works, I, 310. Ames to Gore, December 13, 1802.

elections of 1801 gave further proof of this fact. Early
in the spring the *Columbian Centinel* recorded that for
some time Rhode Island had been "degenerating to its
former 'Know Ye' grade" and had again "arrived at
the nadir of politics."[3] The Republicans secured a
majority in the legislature and voted an address to
President Jefferson.[4] Republicanism had conquered its
first New England state. The President was aware of
the significance of this event and on May 3 wrote to
Granger: "A new subject of congratulation has arisen.
I mean the regeneration of Rhode Island. I hope it is
the beginning of that resurrection of the genuine spirit
of New England which rises for life eternal. According
to natural order, Vermont will emerge next, because
least, after Rhode Island, under the yoke of hierarchy."[5]
For the next six years the state offers little of political
interest. Arthur Fenner was re-elected governor almost
without opposition—except in 1802—until his death in
1805.[6] Then, after a deadlock in 1806, due to the want
of a popular majority, his son, James Fenner, succeeded
to the chair. To the Federalists the state was "a wart
on the body of New England"; "given to idols, let her
alone," expresses their attitude.[7] It took an event like

3 April 22, 1801. *Ibid.*, May 16. A letter from Providence remarks
dolefully: "We have but one consolation that at present by the constitution they cannot make paper money, for if they could we should apprehend
the validity of contracts and I fear the suspension of business as in
1786. . . . The legislature adjourned yesterday afternoon and almost all
the federal men throughout the state who were judges and held offices of
any consequence are removed and Jacobins substituted."

4 Rhode Island Schedules, 1801, 21.

5 FORD, Jefferson Writings, VIII, 48.

6 In 1802 William Greene was the Federal candidate. Fenner won by
a vote of 3802 to 1934. Providence Phœnix, May 11.

7 Col. Centinel, February 19, 1803.

In November, 1801, Rhode Island observed her emancipation from Federalism by refusing to appoint a day of Thanksgiving, the latter custom
savoring too much of the "presbyterian tyranny" of Massachusetts.

the laying of the embargo to shake the state out of its apathy.

Jefferson's belief that Vermont would be the first to follow Rhode Island's example proved correct. The fall election gave the Republicans a majority in the legislature and an address to the President was adopted by a vote of eighty-six to fifty-nine.[8] In the previous session the Federalists had had a majority of more than thirty. Isaac Tichenor, it is true, was still governor, but that office meant little more than the honor of presiding in the council meetings.[9] Tichenor continued to hold office, although by lessening majorities until 1807. As in the case of Rhode Island, state politics in Vermont have little interest in these years.

Connecticut offered a less promising field for the new party than any of the other states but even here it made steady gains during the early years of the century. In 1801 the Republicans met in Wallingford to celebrate the inauguration of Jefferson, and soon after, a caucus at Norwalk put a state ticket in the field, including a candidate for governor.[10] This was practically the first time that opposition had been offered to Governor Trumbull and was therefore a portentous event. "Everything dear and respectable is now openly attacked," the *Courant* recorded.[11] Trumbull received 11,156 votes in a total of 13,307, an apparently unprom-

Abstracts of speeches made in the legislature on this occasion are found in Conn. Courant, November 16. Col. Centinel, November 25. "Tomorrow will be observed as a day of Thanksgiving and praise throughout this state, New Hampshire, and Connecticut, and by such of the citizens of Rhode Island as have the grace to thank God for anything."

[8] Records of Governor and Council, IV, 497.

[9] N. H. Gazette, September 2, 1806, describes Tichenor as "the present milk-sop, half way federal Governor."

[10] Conn. Courant, April 6, 1801.

[11] *Ibid.*

ising start for Republicanism.[12] But there was evidence that this was not a fair party test. There were more than thirty Republicans in the legislature, and popular gains in the party were reported to be taking place all over the state.[13] In any case there was enough progress in the movement to excite alarm among the Federalists and at the fall session of the legislature a bill for regulating elections was introduced, a measure which the Republicans charged was aimed directly at their growing numbers. By this law the justices of the peace were made presiding officers in all electoral assembles and oral voting substituted for vote by ballot. As the justices were appointed by the Federalist majority in the legislature, and were in many cases themselves candidates for election, the Republicans felt that their opponents by giving the justices such powers were simply entrenching themselves to insure a majority. The Republicans fought the passage of the bill and on their defeat drew up a protest which was spread through the state.[14]

Republicanism gained slowly but surely. The number of members in the legislature rose to seventy-eight in 1804, the greatest strength attained in this period.[15] The vote for governor grew in like proportion. The

12 *Ibid.*, May 19.

13 Am. Mercury, June 11, 1801. Contains an interesting article on the growth of Republicanism, including a list of towns which were ''becoming convinced that Federalism is a delusion.''

14 An account of the passage of the bill, and the protest of the minority appears in Am. Mercury, November 5, 1801. For the Federalist side, Conn. Courant, November 9. A mock protest appears in which it is stated that under the old system of balloting, ''the Republican candidate has obtained many hundred votes which persons would have been ashamed to give had they been known. The freemen will blush to vote for Potter,'' etc.

15 Col. Centinel, October, 1804, gives numbers of Republicans in Connecticut House: October, 1801, 40; May, 1802, 55; October, 1803, 75; May, 1804, 78.

Republicans of Bristol County, Massachusetts, in 1804, in an address which reviewed New England political conditions, referred to this state as follows: "In Connecticut truth and reason are pervading the mass of the people. A hallowed jealousy is shaking their bigoted assembles and the pontifical chair of the clergy totters beneath them."[16] This was perhaps an optimistic view, but Republicanism was unquestionably stirring the political life of the state as it had never been stirred before. In Connecticut, unlike the other states, the Republicans had a somewhat radical program. A more liberal suffrage, constitutional reform, and, above all, religious liberty, were questions brought before the public between 1801 and 1804. In the legislature, debates were long and acrimonious and the rival newspapers were filled with scurrilous attacks on party leaders. But Federalism retained control of the state almost unshaken. Connecticut was essentially conservative.[17] The Federalist administration of the state had been economical and honest; the older leaders still retained the respect of the people; the clergy and the bar used their influence against all forms of innovation. The property qualification and the election law may have helped, but probably Connecticut remained Federalist because the majority of the people were satisfied to vote as they had always voted.[18] The statement of the *Courant* that "Connecticut can never be disorganized,

[16] Ind. Chronicle, March 15, 1804.

[17] Republican Watchtower, July 27, 1801. "That Connecticut compared to her sister states, possesses a vast mass of prejudice is a fact generally admitted. . . . The ambition of her leading characters overleaps republican bounds."

[18] A good summary of Connecticut's political history for this period is J. C. WELLING, Connecticut Federalism, in Addresses, lectures and other papers. Cambridge, Mass., 1904. See also, GREENE, Religious Liberty in Conn.

revolutionized, or demoralized, except at a thin freeman's meeting" seems to have been based on real
facts.[19]

Next to Connecticut, Massachusetts offered the most
stubborn resistance to Republicanism. Like the people
of the former state, her inhabitants were slow in changing their habits. In the pre-revolutionary days "ten
years of strenuous opposition were required to convince
people that Hutchinson was an enemy of rights and
liberty."[20] Boston, the intellectual and commercial
center of New England, became the political headquarters of the leading Federalists, who maintained in this
stronghold an almost fanatical opposition to Jefferson
and his party.[21] Hampshire, the great interior county
of the state, was also an area of pronounced conservatism.[22]

But unlike Connecticut, the state had, as has been
noted, a well-developed party system. The Republicans had also a group of leaders, not equal to the Federalists it is true, but nevertheless of considerable
ability. Eustis, Varnum, Gerry, Dearborn, Lincoln,
Sullivan, were probably the best known and ablest of
the New England Republicans. Federalism never
had the complete dominance which it enjoyed in Connecticut and only by desperate exertions was it able to
hold its own.

The attempt to displace Governor Strong did not meet

19 April 6, 1801.

20 Ind. Chronicle, April 9, 1804.

21 AMORY, Life of James Sullivan, II, 123. The Ind. Chronicle, November 22, 1804, describes the political power of Boston as due to the influence of bank interests, British agents, old and young tories, shopkeepers
obtaining English credit, insurance companies, the state officials, and
"Essex and Plymouth men who have taken refuge in the reservoir of
aristocracy."

22 MORSE, Fed. Party in Mass., 180.

with much success. His majorities over Gerry grew steadily until 1803. But while this was the case, the number of Republicans in the legislature increased.[23] The year 1803 was characterized by lack of interest and a light vote, but 1804 brought back the vigor and acrimony of 1800. The Republicans nominated Attorney-General James Sullivan. The campaign was sharply contested and the vote much heavier than in the preceding year. Strong was re-elected by a majority of about six thousand, while the Republicans made decided gains in the legislature.[24]

A remarkable change took place in the District of Maine. Until 1803 Federalism had had a decided majority, the people being considered "peaceable and honest federalists."[25] In the election of this year, however, the Republicans made a gain of over four thousand votes, practically wiping out Strong's majority of 1803.[26] The Republican majorities increased rapidly during the next few years and the party maintained continuous control of the District throughout the period under discussion. As this is practically the only striking party change in the period it is worth some examination.

There had been for some time a certain friction between Massachusetts proper and the District. The latter was essentially a frontier country with a rapidly

[23] The votes for Speaker in the House stood in favor of the Federalists: 1802, 110 to 47; 1803, 124 to 73; 1804, 129 to 103. N. H. Gazette, June 12, 1804.

[24] Strong, 30,007; Sullivan, 23,979. Col. Centinel, May 16.

[25] Spooner's Vermont Journal, March 27, 1804. Quoted from Political Barometer. New Hampshire is described as "a federal but not factious state" and as having "more honest federalism than any other state in the Union."

[26] For interesting comments on this change see Ind. Chronicle, June 10. The Eastern Argus, November 30, gives a summary of the various elections of the year.

growing population. There was a feeling that the older part of the state neglected the interests of Maine, and this found expression in attempts to bring about a separation, those of 1788, 1792, and 1797 being perhaps the most noteworthy. The agitation never fully subsided, although it was not at this time made a party issue.[27] The people of the District complained of an inadequate judicial system and other disadvantages due to their distance from the capital.[28]

But there was a more serious grievance which early in the century aroused the antagonism of the two sections and had important political consequences. After the close of the Revolution and later, the government disposed of large tracts of public land to individuals and corporations. The settlers who were moving rapidly into the new territory often settled on these proprietary grants, made improvements, and then found themselves liable to eviction or prosecution as trespassers. In many cases the proprietors were unable or unwilling to give titles to those who claimed them.[29] The result was a great deal of confusion and ill feeling. The proprietors were regarded as oppressors and acts of violence against them and their surveyors occasionally took place.

The bearing of this matter on the political situation resembles that of the Langdon bank on the politics of New Hampshire. The feeling of dissatisfaction in Maine was growing in force during the years 1800-1804. In the latter year the governor urged that measures be taken against trespassers in the District[30] and soon after

[27] STANWOOD, Separation of Maine from Massachusetts, Proceedings Mass. Hist. Soc., 3d Series, I, 136-138.

[28] Ibid., 129.

[29] WILLIAMSON, History of Maine, II, 583-584, 592.

[30] House Journal, XXV, 165, 195.

this, events in the legislature seemed to identify Federalism with the proprietary interests.

The history of this business was used as campaign material by the *Eastern Argus,* established in 1803 as the first Republican paper in the District. In 1805, at the spring session of the legislature, a motion was made by William King to inquire into the way in which the corporations or individual grantees had fulfilled the conditions of their contracts. When it was found that they had not properly carried out the terms of the grants a resolve authorizing the attorney-general to begin suit against delinquents was passed by the House. In the Senate, David Cobb, the president, who was agent for the Bingham claims, was said to have used his influence to bring about the defeat of the measure.[31] The settlers were deeply aggrieved at the failure of the proprietors to place additional settlers, as required by the terms of many grants, or to issue titles to those who actually occupied land. The refusal of the Federalists in the legislature to require the Pejepscot proprietors, some of the worst offenders, to place settlers, was regarded as a gross abuse of party power, the proprietors being mostly prominent Federalists of Newburyport and Newbury.[32]

There was no doubt that the land question made an excellent issue on which to appeal to the settlers. An election address in 1804, on behalf of Orchard Cook, then running for Congress in the Lincoln district, cites that "he is a friend to the hardy settlers of the forest, and opposed to the oppressive demands of those who lay yearly contributions on the inhabitants without

---

[31] See ALLEN, Bingham Land. Coll. of Me. Hist. Soc., VII, 356. E. Argus, October 11, 1804, August 30, 1805, April 11, March 28, 1806, March 26, 1807.

[32] *Ibid.,* March 28, 1806.

offering a title to support their claims.''[33] A similar
address by Nathan Weston, a candidate for the council
two years later, complains that Massachusetts was interested solely in the profits of the sales and urges the
sale of land in small lots to real settlers only.[34] Says
another electioneering document:

> Let your towns be represented, and let it be their care to
> arrest the selling of our lands in large tracts to idle specula-
> tors, to supercilious Lordlings, whose haughtiness, folly, and
> vanity you find on trial to be so insufferable. If you look well
> to your interests, the time is not far distant, when you may
> make such just laws for the limitation of real actions, that
> Tom Piper shall not be able to drive you from your settlements,
> under the pretence that Jack Pudding sold the whole soil for
> a Keg of Rum, or the State for a Cent an Acre. The evils, of
> which our settlers have so justly complained would probably
> have been long since remedied, had they had friends in Court.[35]

Such appeals were undoubtedly effective. To the
settler in the wilderness, the title to land was one of
the great objects of life. The idea that the Federalists
in Boston, hundreds of miles away, were responsible for
their difficulties was intolerable. There need be no surprise that in 1804 it is reported ''There is a revolutionary spirit of politics operative in the province of
Maine.''[36] The importance of the land question was
fully recognized at the time. The Federalists complained that ''demagogues'' were urging the settlers to
defeat Governor Strong, in order to avert wholesale
evictions.[37] The results of elections in 1804, 1805, and
1806 showed the effectiveness of this campaign. Even

---

[33] E. Argus, November 1, 1804.
[34] Ibid., April 11, 1806.
[35] Ibid., July 5, 1805.
[36] Portland Gazette, December 24, 1804.
[37] Ibid., May 12, 1806.

General Knox was beaten in 1804 by Joshua Adams, a blacksmith, the objection to him being that he owned too much land, and "A great land holder is a kind of natural Aristocrat."[38] The Federalist belief was that "mere politics had very little influence in changing the District of Maine,"[39] but in any case the change was of great importance and had a vital influence on Massachusetts politics.[40] The Republicans in the state proper now had a powerful auxiliary in the district, and the alliance enabled them for the first time to break down the power of the Federalist party. The widespread belief that "the patentee is not the proper person to legislate for the squatter" led to a demand that the Maine towns send more representatives to the legislature in order to protect their interests.[41]

The result of the political revolution in Maine was to give the Republicans an even chance of victory in the state at large. The election of 1805 further reduced

[38] E. Argus, August 30, 1805.

[39] Portland Gazette, May 12, 1806.

[40] AMES, Works, I, 310. "The District of Maine grows yearly worse and worse. If that part of the state could stand neuter Massachusetts proper would be right some years longer. Either we ought to dismember that territory—or we should make the most unremitted exertions to Federalize it." Ames to Pickering, March 10, 1806.

The Federalists expressed resentment at the loss of power by this means. Col. Centinel, April 30, 1806. "Shall the Squatters of Maine impose a governor on Massachusetts?" A Fourth of July toast in Boston in the same year, "Old Massachusetts—may it soon be purified from the dross of Maine, and so become the brightest link in the golden chain of our union." E. Argus, July 10.

Further Republican resentment was caused by the Federalist attempt to disfranchise the plantations—largely in Maine. AMORY, Sullivan, II, 162.

[41] E. Argus, July 5, 1805. A bill to pay town representatives from the state treasury, defeated February 10, 1807, was probably a measure intended to favor the Maine representatives. The vote was 178 to 75 against it. The vote of the Maine delegation was 43 to 21 in favor. House Journal, XXVII, 379.

Governor Strong's majority[42] and for a while the election of 1806 seemed to have given the state to the Republicans. After a long canvass of the returns it was finally decided that Strong was elected, but the other branches of the government were Republican.[43] The campaigns of this year and of the following year were exceedingly bitter, but the Republicans were now the winning party and Sullivan was elected governor by over two thousand majority in 1807. The result was received with great satisfaction by Republicans throughout the country.[44] The legislature in its winter session had already passed a vote of confidence in the President.

Federalism had not such a hold on New Hampshire. As has been seen, a vigorous opposition to Gilman's administration sprang up in 1800. The Republican candidate, Walker, was replaced in 1802 by John Langdon, whose long record of public service was a decided asset to his party. Gilman's majority fell to about sixteen hundred.[45] In the legislature the Federalists had a majority of four in the Senate and about twenty in the House. Two years later Gilman succeeded by but seventy-four votes and the Republicans controlled the legislature.[46] The conquest of New Hampshire was more rapid than that of Massachusetts and in the following year Langdon won by the decisive majority of 3810.[47] The collapse of the Federalist party in this year is interesting. In 1806 Langdon polled 15,277 in a total vote of 20,573, although the fact that about eight thou-

[42] FORD, Jefferson Writings, VIII, 354. To Sullivan, May 21, 1805. "Another year restores Massachusetts to the general body of the nation."

[43] STANWOOD, The Massachusetts Election in 1806. Proceedings Mass. Hist. Soc., 2d Series, XX, 12.

[44] See quotations in Ind. Chronicle, June 8, 1807.

[45] Gilman, 10,377; Langdon, 8753. Col. Centinel, June 5, 1802.

[46] N. H. Gazette, June 12, 1804. The total vote was 24,452.

[47] Ibid., June 11, 1805.

sand less votes were cast in this year than in 1805 shows that there was a large body of voters which could become formidable to the Republicans if again brought to the polls.[48]

In national politics Republicanism made great gains although not as complete as in the state. Connecticut and New Hampshire adhered to the general ticket system, the former sending, under the apportionment of 1801, seven representatives, the latter five. The former of course sent only Federalists. New Hampshire first sent a Republican delegation in 1806. Rhode Island's two representatives were also chosen by general ticket and were Republicans in each case. Vermont had used the district system, the state for several terms electing one Federalist and one Republican. Under the new apportionment the state was allowed four members. In 1802 the delegation was evenly divided, in the two succeeding elections the Republicans had three of the four members. Massachusetts now had seventeen members; by 1806 eleven of the number were Republicans, the Federalists retaining their hold only on north Essex, Suffolk, Hampshire, and Worcester.

The presidential election of 1804 showed remarkable Republican strength. In Massachusetts the Federalists in the legislature were apparently unwilling to arouse the ill feeling of 1800 by again appointing electors themselves. Accordingly, the vote was given to the people, the electors to be voted on by general ticket. This was received with scant enthusiasm by the Repub-

[48] Portsmouth Oracle, June 14, 1806. In his message the governor mentioned that differences in political sentiments were fast subsiding.

Ibid., September 6, in reference to congressional elections, ''In regard to the late election, nobody appears to have any interest in it except the candidates themselves.''

See also Col. Centinel, March 15, 1806.

licans who had demanded a vote by district.[49] The
result, however, was a general surprise, for the Republicans carried the state. In New Hampshire there was
a similar result, the Republican electoral ticket being
successful where their congressional ticket had failed
a few weeks earlier.[50] Vermont and Rhode Island gave
their votes to Jefferson, the former state electing
through the legislature,[51] the latter by popular vote on
general ticket.[52]

By 1807, then, the Republicans were in full control
of the governments of four New England states, and
they had also a majority of the members of Congress.
Governor Trumbull in Connecticut was the only Federalist of importance who still held state office. The
change during the last seven years had been sweeping,
and yet had few revolutionary characteristics. Maine
was the only region which showed a sudden and complete
change in political opinion.

There is a noticeable lack of local issues in all the
states except Connecticut and there Federalism held its
own. Parties were now on a national basis and national
affairs until the latter part of Jefferson's second administration offered no issues which could be brought home
to people as were the revenue or sedition measures of
1798. The personal element was of course a strong factor, and the reliance on such eminently "safe" men as

[49] Col. Centinel, June 9, 16, 1804. The protests of the Senate and House
minorities were published June 20.

[50] The votes in 1804 stood: Governor, Federalist, 12,216, Republican,
12,039; Electoral, Federalist, 8386, Republican, 9083; Congressional, Federalist, 10,881, Republican, 10,455. Col. Centinel, September 12, 1804.

In Massachusetts the vote stood: Governor, Federalist, 29,197, Republican, 23,755; Electoral, Federalist, 25,139, Republican, 29,254. Ind.
Chronicle, November 15, 22, 1804.

[51] Records of Governor and Council, V, 88.

[52] Col. Centinel, July 4, 1804.

Tichenor, Trumbull, or Strong gave the Federalists a strength which was not shown in other parts of the government.

Appeals to the voters in New Hampshire and Massachusetts where the struggle was closest and most exciting show few traces of a definite party program. There is a great deal of talk about the comparative dangers of aristocracy and democracy and an endless variety of personal attacks, such as those on Sullivan, whom the Federalists charged with numerous sharp practices.[53] A Republican address of 1804 attacks Strong for his subservience to the Essex Junto; men of "Hamilton monarchic tendencies" and "friends of standing armies and the funding system."[54] In New Hampshire, electioneering documents have a similar tone. Gilman was upheld as a faithful public servant who should not be turned out; his opponents urged that he had held office long enough and that it was time for a change—"the pernicious principle of rotation," as the Federalists styled this argument.[55]

But national matters formed the basis of most of the party appeals and here the Republicans had the popular arguments. The Federalists might lament the defenseless condition of the coast, the destruction of the navy, the repeal of the Judiciary Act, but none of these measures would make an unfavorable impression on the majority of the voters. The noisy demonstration of the leading Federalists in 1804 against the Louisiana purchase, and the sweeping victory of the Republicans in the same year show how little public feeling was aroused against this act of the President. The general prosperity of Jefferson's first administration reacted

[53] AMORY, Sullivan, II, 142-156.
[54] Ind. Chronicle, March 1, 4, 1804.
[55] Portsmouth Oracle, February 20, 1802.

strongly in favor of his party. "The people do not believe that prudence and economy in the national government are criminal or that they are all going to be ruined because they have no taxes to pay," says an address to the voters of New Hampshire.[56] The real weakness and folly of some features of the Jeffersonian régime were soon to be demonstrated, however popular it was in 1804.

Why did Massachusetts vote for Jefferson? [asks the *American Mercury* in 1804]. The Federalists pretend it is only a temporary departure from the old school. The change has arrived as the similar change has arrived in other states. The federalists traded too powerfully under Mr. Adams on the strength of three votes majority. . . . They foretold the wicked things the new President would do, and he has not done them. . . . People know the difference between a government aimed for their good and a government aimed at the exclusive glory of the rulers. . . . The majority of the people have discovered that their federalists did not possess the piety, talents, or political integrity which they claimed.[57]

The significance of Republican growth in these seven years is shown by later events. There was now an evenly balanced party system throughout the region. One party was almost wholly sectional, the other, national. Had the Federalists maintained their predominance of 1798, the history of the Union would probably have been changed by the events of 1808 to 1815. For the next seven years Republicanism was able for the most part, to counterbalance the dangerous tendencies of Federalism.

56 N. H. Gazette, August 7, 1804.
57 December 6, 1804.

CHAPTER IV

PARTY METHODS

The spread of "Republican light and truth" or of "the wicked and subversive principles of Jacobinism," to use the terms of supporters or opponents of the movement, was not, of course, wholly spontaneous. Education and organization played the same vitally important part that they have in the growth of other political parties. The obstacles to the development of a new party were formidable. Political indifference has already been discussed; poor means of travel and communication and expensive printing were additional factors. Besides these, the excessive localism of town organization and the influence of its clerical and political leaders covered New England with Federalist redoubts which could only be captured by long continued and scientific sapping and mining. For such operations regulars were needed as well as militia.

In any discussion of party organization and methods in this period certain facts must be kept in mind. The conception of party and its functions at the opening of the nineteenth century was, at least on the part of the Federalists, essentially different from our own. The modern idea of party as an association of citizens aiming at the expression of legislative or administrative policies through control of governmental machinery had not yet been accepted. Perhaps the attitude of the Federalists on this question constitutes the best evidence on the existence of class rule. To them, political organization meant conspiracy, and party an unmixed evil. Opposition was aimed, not at policies, but at institutions. "Insurgents" is the term applied by William Plumer to the first Republicans appearing in New Hampshire.[1] Throughout the period Federalists looked back longingly to the Golden Age before state or town was disrupted by electioneering. Typical of this attitude are utterances in the Massachusetts *Mercury* in 1800. "It is to be regretted that parties are inseparable from all free governments but like all human enjoyments, liberty must have its alloy. . . . Naturally there can be but two parties in a Country; the friends of order and its foes. Under the banners of the first are ranged all men of property, all quiet, honest, peaceable, orderly, unambitious citizens. In the ranks of the last are enlisted all desperate, embarrassed, unprincipled, disorderly, ambitious, disaffected, morose men."[2] In the writings of the party leaders, in their sermons, pamphlets, and newspapers the same idea is constantly found.

Less familiar than those of Cabot, Ames, or Pickering, the ideas of William Plumer are as typical of Federalist sentiment. The grant or refusal of commercial charters for political reasons has not disappeared from American politics, but it would take a politician of sturdier breed than now appears at our state capitals to stand on the floor of the House and oppose the grant of a bank charter for the reasons he urged in 1800. "The memorialists have established a Gazette called the Ledger, the very soul of which is opposition to the

[1] MSS., I, 288. Plumer to Smith, March 9, 1796.

[2] Quoted by N. H. Gazette, August 26, 1800. Cf. E. Argus, March 16, 1804. "It is customary with some to call the free exercise of Popular Suffrage, Revolutionizing, and every change in the Officers of Government, tho' effected by suffrage only, a Revolution." Quoted from Political Observatory.

administration. That this paper is the vehicle of the vilest slander and the most virulent calumny against men in office. . . . Its columns are filled with extracts from the most false and filthy publications that disgrace the Aurora, the Press, the Times, the Telegraphe and other papers established for the avowed purpose of effecting a revolution of the State and general government.'' To incorporate these men as a banking society would be to give them ''the means of extending their political poison with more certain success''; it would ''furnish our internal enemies with arms against ourselves,'' particularly when in the last election ''they employed runners through the state to oppose the election of the present governor and every federal councillor, senator and representative.''[3] Two years later, showing the reluctance of Federalists to recognize the passing of the old order, he writes that while ''the minds of many people appear in a state of fermentation and discover a strong inclination to effect a change in their rulers,'' yet ''if our Republican government can be supported for a few years more, I fondly hope this unreasonable spirit of jealousy and distrust of men in office will subside. That the people will see that the principal motive that influences the conduct of our fault finders is to obtain offices not to diminish public expenses—and that they will again return to their old sober habits of life & venerate the men of their former choice.''[4]

The attitude toward party organization and campaign practices is similar. The Republicans were held responsible for such innovations. ''While abusing Great Britain,'' says one writer, ''they copy there, abuses of

[3] MSS., I, 425. Plumer to Smith, June 14, 1800, giving a summary of his speech in the legislature.
[4] *Ibid.*, 449. Plumer to Upham, June 27, 1802.

the true freedom of election. Until recently elections in New England were free beyond any example to be found elsewhere." In the strictest sense officers were chosen by the people, bribery was unknown, and "it was imprudent to express a wish for promotion," as merit could alone bring political success. "Unhappily our democrats have already had some influence in changing this truly republican state of things" and "the detestable practise of electioneering is coming in," copied by the South from Great Britain and from there brought into New England.[5]

The effect of the above attitude toward party and party machinery is readily seen. Organization and electioneering were forced under cover; when detected they were admitted to be outside the accepted rules of the game but justifiable as measures of retaliation. The student of the subject finds his task made heavier and he is forced to glean most of his knowledge from an occasional circular or broadside and from the prejudiced comment of opposing newspapers.

Prior to the advent of the Republicans there is little information as to party machinery and it continues scanty until after 1800. In the earlier period, various factors made needless an extensive organization; indifference, the narrow range of political interest, the long terms of public officers. People could be trusted to accept the candidates offered by informal conferences of the leaders. The lack of organized effort is seen in the large number of candidates frequently offered and

[5] Conn. Courant, February 2, 1801. Cf. Mass. Spy, May 11, 1803. "Villicus." "The newspapers whose columns were once adorned and made highly useful to the perusers by moral and religious essays are now crowded with vile aspersions against men and measures. Elections were once conducted with decorum and unanimity: respect was paid to such men, only, as were distinguished for their probity and talents. Now they have become the objects of intrigue, the time for contentions and strife."

the difficulty of securing a majority for any one.[6] Campaigning was the work of guerillas rather than disciplined organizations, the "itinerant Jacobins" of 1792 or the "runners" mentioned by Plumer.[7] Conditions rapidly change, however, after 1800. Within a few years both parties were organized and disciplined along practically the same lines.

Among the objects of party organization, Mr. Bryce remarks, are the nomination of candidates, the promotion of unity, inspiring enthusiasm and energy, and the education of the voter with a view to adding him to the party ranks. The first of these objects was secured by the establishment of what is probably the most powerful and important piece of party machinery to be found in this period, the legislative caucus. It is found in active operation in Rhode Island as early as 1790, and it is very probable that in all the states leaders would take advantage of their presence at the capital to discuss future action. Events of 1800, however, gave this body vastly greater importance. It would have been, under any conditions, a powerful institution. Communication was slow and difficult and it would have been hard indeed on any other occasion to have secured

[6] LUETSCHER, Early Political Machinery, 121. In 1800 there were reported to be "nearly a dozen" candidates contesting the Vermont eastern district. Mass. Spy, October 8, 1800.

[7] MSS., I, 161. Plumer to Foster, June 28, 1790. "The people appear divided & trifles light as air unite and divide them, Runners are active, many of whom are unprincipled rascals." See also 283 (1796) and 410 (1800). Also cf. 211, Page to Plumer, June 26, 1792. "All was confusion—the parties were not formed for electing members to Congress & were so much afraid of each other that they strove only to conceal themselves & their designs."

The Conn. Journal, April 4, 1799, states, "Your democratic literati, so often at houses of public entertainment harangue the mob, and with unparalleled effrontery insult the understanding and weary the patience of the traveler."

a meeting of so many persons from such widely separated parts of the state.[8] Then, too, its members were
influential men in their own localities who would go
home ready to carry out the plans decided on in the
meeting. A contemporary defense of the Vermont
Republican caucus says: "It cannot be denied that information respecting the candidates for office is necessarily
to be obtained by some means or other, unless every
man would vote for the inhabitants of his own town or
neighborhood only, which is contrary to the nature of
our government, and information from representatives
of the people and other eminent characters who usually
attend the legislature is generally the most correct that
can be obtained."[9]

It did not, however, receive full approbation as is
indicated by the apologetic tone adopted in the addresses
issued to the public. A Federalist defense of the Massachusetts caucus of 1800, in reply to the charge that they
were dictating to the voters, explains that its members
met "not in their legislative capacity," but merely as
citizens interested in a common cause "to discuss the
merits of certain persons" as candidates, while in spite
of their outcry the Jacobins had met the same evening
"in an obscure room in the easterly part of Boston."[10]
An address issued by the Federalist caucus in Connecticut in 1803 admits that the meeting and the address
constitute "a deviation from the ancient practice of the
state" but are rendered necessary by the growing
activity of their opponents.[11] In functions and meth-

---

[8] Political meetings in this period were frequently held when court was
in session in order to take advantage of the presence of the crowd. See
E. Argus, February 24, 1806; BENTLEY, Diary, III, 359; National Aegis,
September 24, 1806; Vt. Republican, May 11, 1812.

[9] Spooner's Vt. Journal, March 17, 1806.

[10] Mass. Spy, March 26, 1800.

[11] Conn. Courant, June 8, 1803. The same apologetic attitude toward

ods there seems to have been no difference between the caucuses of the two parties, except that Republicans claimed to be free from the secrecy which characterized their opponents. Thus a comparison of the two legislative caucuses held at Rutland, Vt., in 1804, states that the Republicans met believing it a fair way of learning the public mind and "the most potent antidote against private electioneering" and published the results of their deliberations, while at the same time about thirty Federalists met under a solemn agreement to secrecy. "The Federalists industriously circulate stories against caucuses, and the very idea of caucuses has alarmed many people."[12] The New Hampshire situation is described thus: "Their caucusses have differed from our conventions in these particulars—theirs have been extremely *secret,* while ours have been *open*—theirs have been in the night, ours in the day, a few *only* (the well born) have been admitted to theirs—to ours all who pleased to attend."[13] Federalist hypocrisy in the matter of party organization is constantly denounced by their opponents.[14]

the caucus is seen in the following comment on the New Hampshire caucus. N. H. Gazette, June 3, 1806. "It is said there will be no legislative caucussing the present session.—The Republican cause stands on such firm ground that the people may be safely trusted with the selection of proper candidates for office, without other guidance or influence than their own judgment. Legislative Caucussing has been always opposed, but defended on the principle of necessity; if that necessity no longer exists, the dangerous and alarming practice will be laid aside."

[12] Quoted from Vt. Gazette by Pol. Observatory, October 19, 1805. Reference to preceding year.

[13] *Ibid.,* March 9, 1805; also July 28, 1804. A description of the Federalist system of holding caucuses "in dark chambers, beneath the security of lock and key with permission for none to enter but the initiated." According to this, their legislative caucus met in a Concord schoolhouse at 4 a.m.

[14] See Spooner's Vt. Journal, March 17, 1806; E. Argus, April 6, 1804; Pol. Observatory, April 21, 1804. Salem Register, February 28, 1805. The

The functions of the legislative caucus were very extensive. Its nominating powers were great, and from it originated the powerful committee system that will presently be discussed. In all the states it nominated candidates for the higher executive offices. In Connecticut and Vermont it nominated the councillors, in Rhode Island and in New Hampshire, until 1810, the senators.[15] Where national representatives were chosen by general ticket it also made nominations[16] and at times appears to have made district nominations.[17] When presidential electors were chosen by popular vote the caucus drew up the ticket.[18]

In Massachusetts the power of the caucus over nominations was considerably less. Senators were elected by counties and national representatives by districts, with the result that the county meeting or "convention," as it comes to be styled, is of some importance. Prior to 1800 it seems to have had but slight importance, although making nominations occasionally even then.[19] Its importance grows with the increase in political

following comment of later date may be of interest. Nat'l Aegis, December 25, 1816. "Do they assemble to select a candidate for publick office? It is called a large and respectable Meeting of Federalists. . . . Their conclaves are called 'meetings' and Republican assemblages for similar purposes are styled 'caucuses.' Monroe is selected for the Presidency by a *Caucus*—and Gov. Brooks is proposed as Governor by a *Federal Meeting*."

15 LUETSCHER, Early Political Machinery, 119-124 *passim*. Also see following for statements regarding work of Republican caucuses: Pol. Observatory, August 10, 1805 (Vt.); *Ibid.*, September 14 (Conn.).

Plumer MSS., IV, 123 [In N. H.]. "The democrats held a general caucus and nominated every candidate," J. W. Thompson to Plumer, February 27, 1804.

16 *Ibid.*, I, 428, gives account of New Hampshire caucus of 1800 which nominated ticket of representatives.

17 Spooner's Vt. Journal, November 27, 1804, January 15, 1805. There was considerable opposition to this nomination.

18 Nat'l Aegis, September 5, 1804. Mass. Spy, June 22, 1808.

19 DALLINGER, Nominations for Elective Office in the United States, 23-25.

interest. It was a necessary concession to local feeling.[20] Congressional districts usually coincided with county lines, and in some cases where two districts were included, the county convention nominated candidates for both.[21] For a number of years the county meeting seems to have been little more than a mass meeting to which a general invitation was announced, or special invitations issued by the county committee.[22] It is not surprising to find occasional complaint that its nominations were controlled by a few.[23] The offer of the Suffolk nomination to John Quincy Adams by the party committee has a decidedly modern sound.[24] The mass meeting was gradually replaced by the convention, and although both methods were in use until 1810 the usual reports of Republican nominating assemblies state that they were composed of "delegates."[25] The county mass

[20] The E. Argus, April 5, 1805, states that the Federalists were trying to discredit the Republican senatorial ticket in York County by circulating handbills charging its nomination by the Boston caucus.

[21] Mass. Spy, October 3, 1804.

[22] Nat'l Aegis, December 12, 1804. March 26, 1806. The invitation to a Bristol congressional district convention is addressed "to all who feel a patriotic interest in the success of Republican principles." Ind. Chronicle, September 27, 1810.

[23] See Republican Farmer in Nat'l Aegis, October 8, 1806, reference to Worcester County caucus. "The proceedings confirmed me in my former opinion that such measures are inconsistent with an unbiassed freedom of election." The business he says was decided by "a certain junto in the town of Worcester, who think they have the right because they live in the shire town to give laws to the whole county."

[24] J. Q. Adams, Memoirs, I, 539.

[25] Boston Patriot, September 5, 1812, advertises call for York County Republican convention "by delegates from the several towns chosen by legal town meeting or otherwise appointed." Ind. Chronicle, August 18, 1812. Notice to Norfolk Republicans, "Choose delegates according to number of representatives in General Court." See also October 26. E. Argus, September 29, 1814, calls for delegations to Lincoln congressional district convention "equal to twice the number of state representatives." See also Nat'l Aegis, October 19, November 8, 1808, February 8, 15, 1809.

meeting was an important method of influencing public opinion and flourished in all the states in such periods of public excitement as occurred during the embargo or in the weeks following the outbreak of the war with England.[26]

The rise of party affected town government as well as the larger units and indicates a considerable change in one of New England's fundamental institutions. In 1798 a writer from Norfolk County, Mass., complains that "the country people this way, in general, never prepare their minds previous to a town meeting" and were therefore under the influence of "their most influential and learned men," particularly the moderator— "the yeomanry ought to prepare their minds and faculties and not place too much confidence in their head man."[27] Three years later, Noah Webster, defending the notorious Stand-up Law before the Connecticut legislature, and opposing vote by ballot because "it will open a door to electioneering," declares, "Our freemen are honest men, and have not been accustomed to bring votes to proxing; they do not know generally when they go whom they shall vote for."[28] Conditions change greatly when the party system develops and party circulars all emphasize the importance of drawing party lines in town meetings.[29] Town caucuses become very common after 1800, nominating candidates and in the larger towns at least appointing committees to distribute votes and urge the claims of their candidates.[30]

[26] Spooner's Vt. Journal, August 1, 1808, reports 500 in attendance at Chittenden meeting. Vt. Republican, April 10, 1809, reports 900 at a Bennington meeting.

[27] N. H. Gazette, November 14, 1798.

[28] Conn. Journal, November 11, 1802.

[29] New England Palladium, May 10, 1803 (Conn. circular). *Ibid.*, March 29. Mass. Spy, December 12, 1804. Spooner's Vt. Journal, August 14, 1809.

[30] Salem Register, March 12, April 2, 1804, May 16, 1805. BENTLEY,

To keep this system of state and local caucuses working smoothly and to insure proper support from the voters necessitated a permanent organization of party workers and this appears between 1800 and 1805. In the Jefferson correspondence there is an interesting letter addressed to Attorney-General Lincoln and signed by twenty-four "deserving Democrats" of Connecticut, urging the removal of Federalist officeholders in that state and giving, incidentally, an outline of what was probably the first formal party organization in New England. "The season has now arrived when it is necessary for us to organize and adopt measures for conveying to our People just sentiments respecting the motives, measures, and objects of the present administration and to obviate the false impressions which the federalists and federal papers have made and are making upon their minds. This organization which will consist of a General Committee, of County Committees, and of Sub-committees in the towns of the State, must be conducted with great fortitude and perseverance, through much labor and expence to an end difficult to be attained but highly important to a republican administration."[31] A similar scheme of organization was adopted in New Hampshire at a legislative caucus held in December, 1803, consisting of "a Grand Committee of Election and Correspondence" and the usual subordinate bodies.[32] "Are we not fallen on evil times? Did

Diary, III, 222. E. Argus, April 6, 1804. Pol. Observatory, July 28, 1804. N. E. Palladium, March 29, 1803. "It is certain that the Democrats in some of our country towns held caucusses and distributed their votes previous to election."

[31] Jefferson Papers, 2d Series, LII, No. 6. Dated Hartford, June 4, 1801. Among the signatures are those of Kirby, Potter, Edwards, and other Republican leaders.

[32] Col. Centinel, February 29, 1804. Ind. Chronicle, February 23, 1804. See also LUETSCHER, Early Political Machinery, 122.

you believe fifteen years ago that a thing of this kind could happen in New England?'' wrote Jeremiah Smith to Plumer.[33] The latter, however, himself organized the Federalists along similar lines within a few months. ''Democracy at this period,'' says one writer describing the activities of the Massachusetts organization, ''is as awful in consequences as it is novel and insinuating in operations. . . . The leaders although in some respects visionary, are practical men in their indefatigable industry to obtain proselytes.'' The same means used with success in New York, Pennsylvania and Virginia are now introduced into New England. The names of those to be relied on are recorded, the most influential individuals are put on committees, the whole constituting ''an ascending series from country tavern junto up to the great caucus of caucusses in Virginia. What must be the desperate intentions of those, who have, as it were, thus systematized disorganization, and arrayed the foibles, the passions, shall I add, the vices of man in a warfare and conspiracy against all that is reputable and praiseworthy in society?''[34]

Extreme centralization marked all the Republican organizations. The general committee appointed the county committees and they the town committees, and the subordinate units were strictly accountable to their superiors.[35] This centralization of authority probably

[33] Plumer MSS., IV, 101. Smith to Plumer, February 22, 1804. This also gives a summary of the Republican organization.

[34] N. E. Palladium, May 10, 1803.

[35] N. E. Palladium. See ''Instructions'' issued by Republican general committee of Connecticut for the elections of 1801 and 1802, in which an elaborate system of inspection and report is outlined. See also for information on Massachusetts organization, Mass. Spy, May 15, June 12, 1805, March 26, 1806. An outline of the Vermont organization is given in Spooner's Vt. Journal, August 7, 1809, including a ''Grand Inspector'' for the counties on either side of the Green Mountains. In Plumer MSS.,

reached its height in Connecticut when, on the ground that "formerly responsibility was too much divided," the system was reorganized in 1805. A "state manager" was appointed by the general caucus with power to appoint and remove the "county managers," who in turn were directed to appoint in each town "an active, influential, republican manager, who will assure you verbally or in writing that he will faithfully discharge his trust."[36] Under such a system truth is evident in the Federalist comment that the entire system of nomination would be vested in the managers and, "What is it but taking the affairs of the government entirely from the many, and placing them in the hands of the few?"[37] The Federalist organization, however, followed in general the same centralized plan.[38]

The operations of these organizations are revealed in the circulars frequently sent by the general committees to their subordinates. "Getting out the vote" was, of course, their most important function and the importance of getting men to freeman's meeting and detaining them there "until the whole business shall have been finished" is constantly urged. Voters were

III, 103, there is a letter from the chairman of New Hampshire organization announcing Plumer's appointment to the chairmanship of a county committee with power "to name a place of rendezvous and summon the members of your committee to meet for the purpose of adopting such plans as the exigency of the case may require." Plumer was now in the Republican party.

[36] Conn. Courant, November 27, 1805.

[37] *Ibid.*

[38] See description of the Massachusetts Federalist organization by S. E. MORISON, Life of Harrison Gray Otis, I, 290. For contemporary comments, E. Argus, March 21, 1806; Nat'l Aegis, November 19, 1806, March 21, 1810; Salem Register, March 28 and February 28, 1805; Pol. Observatory, August 18, 1804. The Federalists of Cheshire County, N. H., are described, N. H. Gazette, September 11, 1804, as employing "immense pecuniary contributions, systematic caucusing, and incredible exertions."

to be listed "assured Republicans," Federalists, and doubtful. The importance of winning the young men is recognized. The circulation of Republican newspapers and pamphlets was to be a regular part of this propaganda.[39] The duties of the committeemen are perhaps nowhere better summarized than in the diary of Nathaniel Ames at the time of his appointment to the Norfolk County committee.[40]

Another function of party organization, the creation of enthusiasm, was not neglected. Political gatherings and celebrations flourished all through this period. The Fourth of March, the anniversary of Jefferson's inauguration, was celebrated with great enthusiasm—not lessened by the fact that it moved their opponents to outbursts of impotent rage. To the Federalists conditions in New England were beginning to resemble those

[39] See Connecticut circulars of 1801, 1802; N. E. Palladium, May 10, 1803; Mass. Spy, October 3, 1804. The Vermont organization directs papers and pamphlets to be sent to the town committees for distribution, and to draw up a special list of young men about to qualify as voters. Spooner's Vt. Journal, August 7, 1809. The Connecticut circular of 1805 contains similar directions. Conn. Courant, November 27, 1805.

[40] August 29, 1808. "At a Convention of Reps. from all the towns in the county of Norfolk—Cohasset excepted [names given] were appointed a County Committee to communicate with the Central Committee of the State [names], and town or subcommittees to watch over the Republican interest both in state and national governments especially as to elections and appointments—convey intelligence—confute false rumors—confirm the wavering in right principles—prevent delusion of weak brethren—and fight that most formidable enemy of civilized men, political ignorance; a task mighty, endless and insuperable without funds to excite support and disseminate the fruits of patriotic genius—and with the most ample funds will prove a Herculean labor, enough to stagger common undertakers to combat the pulpit, the bar, and host of superstitious vanity, pride, and selfish wretches under foreign influence that never had a conception of searching out principles or seeking the truth, and will neither read, see nor hear anything contrary to their own narrow prejudices, wholly actuated by the impulse of the moment.''

> In Pennsylvania, where M'Kean
> Extends his mild and gentle reign,
> Where birds of every sort and feather
> Flock, and at times get drunk together.[41]

The proceedings of these celebrations show little variety. The New Haven celebration of 1803 is typical and included the firing of salutes, a procession, an oration by Pierpont Edwards, music, a public dinner and a ball in the evening.[42] The most striking feature of such gatherings was the public dinner, with its interminable toast list, expressing party sentiment on men and measures. So numerous were the toasts on such occasions that the modern reader is inclined to accept as truth the Federalist description of such an affair,

> They made a most tremendous stir
> Curs'd, swore and quaff'd till half seas o'er.
> Their skins replete could hold no more—
> Then from their tavern out they sallied
> And under air their forces rallied.[43]

Such gatherings, coming as they did shortly before the spring elections, gave an admirable opportunity for active electioneering of which the leaders took full advantage.[44] Indeed, at the Kennebunk celebration in

[41] N. E. Palladium, February 13, 1801.

[42] Conn. Journal, February 24, 1803, gives announcement. Soon after the celebration, a poem in the Conn. Courant thus described the procession:

> And now across the Green
> A motley throng there pours,
> Drunkards and whores,
> And rogues in scores;
> They all rejoice.

[43] N. E. Palladium, March 20, 1801.

[44] This circular invitation to the New Haven celebration states, "We shall meet not only to rejoice, but we shall meet to unite in measures which shall yield further occasions of joy at the next anniversary." See also Mass. Spy, March 30, 1803, for comment on recent celebrations in Massachusetts.

1804, in addition to the festivities of the occasion a senatorial ticket was nominated and a county organization effected.[45] The other great occasion for party celebration was the Fourth of July and, until the Era of Good Feeling, the two parties almost invariably held separate gatherings on this occasion,[46] listened to their own music and oratory, and consumed their own "true natural juice of the lemon, well tempered and mollified with good W. I. rum and loaf sugar."[47] In 1804 the acquisition of Louisiana was generally celebrated among the Republicans, an act which was particularly galling to their opponents.[48] Political clubs and societies were in disrepute and people remembered the storm of disapproval excited by the Democratic societies of 1794. After 1810 a number of social and political clubs appeared, but, with the exception of the Tammany societies of Rhode Island, were of slight importance.[49]

The work of educating the voter depended largely on the press, and the distribution of newspapers and pamphlets was part of the duty of every party worker. There was undoubtedly considerable activity among Republicans prior to the election of Jefferson. In 1798 Matthew Lyon was reported to be sending large numbers of Bache's newspaper and Gallatin's speeches into Connecticut.[50] In 1800 bundles of Virginia papers were reported to have been sent to various residents of the state with a request to distribute them and "dissemi-

[45] E. Argus, March 9, 1804.

[46] Interesting comment on this custom appears in Spooner's Vt. Journal, August 1, 1808.

[47] Pol. Observatory, July 14, 1804.

[48] See "The Chronicles of King Thomas." Conn. Courant, May 16, 1804.

[49] "The Tammany Societies of Rhode Island" is the title of an interesting monograph by M. W. Jernegan, Providence, 1897.

[50] Conn. Courant, April 23.

nate the principles therein inculcated.''[51] ''A dozen papers call'd the Friend of the People sent me,'' writes Nathaniel Ames, ''to go N. & E. I have dispersed also one of my own.''[52]

The power of the press was everywhere recognized. Fisher Ames declared the newspapers were ''a match for any government,'' and it was a recognition of this fact which tempted the Federalists into the folly of the Sedition Law. In 1802 Granger comments in a letter to Jefferson on the scarcity of Republican newspapers observed in his journey north and that it could not please ''one who believes that public opinion will in a great measure be governed by that Vehicle of Intelligence,''[53] and Elbridge Gerry in a letter of earlier date, discussing the danger of dissolution of the Union, remarks that ''the multiplying of republican papers is a measure of the utmost importance.''[54] There was great activity in this line at the opening of the Jeffersonian era.[55] In 1800 the Pittsfield *Sun* and Salem

---

[51] *Ibid.*, March 31, April 2, 1800.

[52] Diary, February 15, 1800.

[53] Jefferson Papers, 2d Series, XXXVI, No. 49. Granger to Jefferson, September 5, 1802.

[54] *Ibid.*, XXXV, No. 120. Gerry to Jefferson, May 4, 1801. Similar sentiments are expressed in a letter of August 15, 1812, 2d Series, XXX-VIII, No. 5.

[55] In the New Year address of 1801 in the Conn. Courant occur the following lines:

> And lo! in meretricious dress,
> Forth comes a strumpet called ''The Press,''
> Whose haggard, unrequested charms
> Rush into every blackguard's arms.
> Ye weak, deluded minds, beware!
> Nought but the outside here is fair!
> Then spurn the offers of her sway
> And kick the loathsome hag away.

The Col. Centinel, March 15, 1800, reports that Republican papers were being established ''from Portsmouth to Savannah.''

Register were established; in the following year the *National Aegis* began issue at Worcester "from the most solemn conviction of the importance of an attempt to check the current of slander which then issued from the only fountain of intelligence within the county"; in 1802 the Providence *Phœnix* became the chief party organ in Rhode Island. In 1803 the *Eastern Argus* was established in Maine and in the same year the *Political Observatory* began the apparently hopeless task of changing the Federalist sentiment of the river counties in New Hampshire. A year earlier the New Hampshire *Gazette* had passed under the control of Republicans and became the principal party organ. By 1804 there were reported to be three Republican presses in Connecticut "throwing additional light into that benighted corner of the earth."[56] The general defeat of the Republicans on the embargo issue in 1808 was followed in 1809 by the establishment of a new group of Republican papers, chief of which were the Boston *Patriot*, the Vermont *Republican*, and the New Hampshire *Patriot*. In spite of these efforts the Federalists had a great advantage in newspapers and in 1810 there were but twenty-three Republican as compared with sixty-six Federalist papers.[57] The political ferment of the time is readily seen in the continual attempts to found newspapers.[58]

Federalist comment best shows the success of this part of the Republican propaganda. In 1801 one writer declares that "along with infidel philosophy and the refusal to enforce laws relating to religion and man-

[56] Pol. Observatory, June 23.

[57] U. S. Census, 1880, VIII, 38, 39. Reprinted from ISAIAH THOMAS, History of Printing. An interesting comparison is also given in Nat'l Aegis, January 17, 1816.

[58] BENTLEY, Diary, III, 54. "The increase of Gazettes is excessive. I have several times attempted to count the whole number, but they

ners'' one of the most powerful causes of ''the rapid decay of our government is a licentious and prostituted press. . . . The effect it has already produced exceeds calculation, and is next to miraculous.''[59] And another writer eight years later: ''The expenses which are incurred and the labor that is exerted to circulate among the people in the Eastern States, the Democratic papers, particularly those which are issued from the new presses of the Boston Patriot, the New Hampshire Patriot, the Anti-Monarchist, and the Vermont Republican, are such as those have no conception of who have not had opportunities of acquiring particular information upon the subject. The business is as much reduced to a system as ever were the operations of the Jacobins in France. Those who can pay as well as not, are expected to pay; but all who are disposed to read are made to read whether they pay or not. The Federalists must look to this, or their day is over. . . .''[60]

appear and disappear and change places so often that the exact number I cannot ascertain.''

Journalistic amenities of the day are illustrated by the following ''Elegiac Lines'' in the Eastern Argus, December 14, 1804, recording the failure of a Federalist contemporary. ''Obituary No. IV.''

> But two years old the creature was,
> A dark complexioned slut
> Filthy and lying all about;
> But now her mouth is shut.

[59] N. E. Palladium, June 9, 1801. See also August 7.

[60] Mass. Spy, October 4, 1809. Essay XV. For further comments on the circulation of newspapers and other literature see Mass. Spy, December 12, 1804, February 13, 1805; N. E. Palladium, May 10, October 11, 1803 (reference to Connecticut); Spooner's Vt. Journal, August 7, 14, 1809; E. Argus, March 21, 1806.

Timothy Dwight put newspaper reading among the vices of men in the new settlements. Travels, IV, 12. ''To be pert; to gamble; to haunt taverns; to drink; to swear; to read newspapers; to talk on political subjects; to manage the affairs of the nation and neglect their own,'' etc. The Nat'l Aegis, May 2, 1804, puts the following into the mouth of a Federalist clergyman: ''Many of you in spite of all the advice and

In spite of the bitterness of politics in this era there is little evidence of disorder or corruption in elections.[61] The amount of attention which the press occasionally gives to trivial incidents at town meeting, a scuffle between heated partisans, the hanging of an effigy, or jeering at the moderator, would seem to show a law-abiding spirit hardly in harmony with the savage tone of political oratory and literature. Two complaints, however, are general, one made by both parties and the other by the Republicans exclusively. Suffrage qualifications existed in the three southern New England states, the local authorities of the towns determining admissions.[62] The strictness of their enforcement,

friendly warnings of your religious and political fathers, have taken and continue to take, and read Jacobin papers, full of all manner of mischief and subtility of the Devil. You think that these will open your eyes and make you as Gods, knowing good and evil. . . . Modern philosophy full of flattery, invites you to reason for yourselves—But the antient bids you put your trust in no such vain delusions, but submit yourselves to those who are over you in the Lord.''

[61] Dr. Ames gives the following picture of an election day in Dedham. Diary, April 7, 1806. ''Every exertion made by the Feds. to obtain Voters every bribe of treating, carriages and arts of delusion practised. Egg rum was admin'd. at F. Ames office his men and waggon loaded with lumber of unprincipled wretches who would sell their lord for 30 glasses of Egg rum.''

See description of election day in Boston, N. E. Palladium, February 10, 1801.

[62] Mass. Constitution of 1780, Ch. I, Sec. II, Art. II. Qualification for electors of senators, any male inhabitant having a freehold estate within the Commonwealth of the annual income value of three pounds, or any estate of the value of sixty pounds. The above property was required to qualify electors of representatives with the added condition that it must lie within the town and the owner must have resided there one year. (Ch. I, Sec. III, Art. IV.)

Under the law of 1802, Chap. 116, Sec. I (General Laws of Massachusetts, Boston, 1823, 12), the list of voters was to be made out by the assessors and revised and corrected by the selectmen.

The Connecticut requirements are given, Acts and Laws of Conn., Hartford, 1805, 217, as a freehold estate of $7 per annum or $134 personal in the general list along with a ''quiet and peaceable Behavior and

however, being a matter of some doubt, the natural result was very frequently a contest by one party to swell its own ranks by indiscriminate admissions and keep additions from those of its opponent. In 1802 a Federalist complaint runs: "The wretched sons of vice and ignorance have nothing to do with our affairs, and are very properly destitute of all political power. Such is our theory—our practice is too much letting the Jacobins introduce illegal voters. . . . The qualification scarcely excludes any and the Jacobins when they interpret this admit all."[63] The Republicans make similar charges and interesting comment on the ability of the Federalists to get out voters who "produce $200 on the day of election" records that every county and town was divided into districts and "subjected to the scrutiny of numerous and industrious committees. Not a single person is left unnoticed, not a single hamlet unexplored. If they are sick they are conveyed to the meeting house almost upon their beds. . . . Property, loaned expressly for the occasion, is put in the hands of indigent brothers."[64] Federalist papers tell with great glee the story of the Connecticut Republican who for a similar purpose deeded property to "a worthless fellow" only to see it at once attached by the latter's creditors.[65] "Persons steeped in poverty were ennobled by federal

Civil Conversation." Under the law of 1801, p. 549, the "Civil Authority and Selectmen of each Town" were required to hold special meetings and "receive and carefully examine all applications for admission" which was granted by majority vote.

For Rhode Island requirements see Public Laws of R. I., Providence, 1798, 114.

[63] N. E. Palladium, January 29, 1802. Similar charge against Salem, Marblehead, and Gloucester, November 12.

[64] Boston Patriot, March 29, 1815. Quoted from Nat'l Aegis.

[65] N. H. Gazette, September 29, 1800. For further reference on these practices see Mass. Spy, December 12, 1804; N. E. Palladium, May 6, 1803 (quoted from Newport Mercury).

act and management, not charity, to claim property on the occasion sufficient to qualify for voting," writes Levi Lincoln to Jefferson.[66]

The second complaint is of some interest as throwing light on the membership of the parties—the constant charge of intimidation brought by Republicans. In the letter already quoted Lincoln brings the charge of "intolerance and oppressive violence in electioneering. Individuals have been threatened with a deprivation of employment and an instant exaction of debt to the last farthing as the consequence of withholding a federal vote, or rather of not giving one." "The Republicans do not appoint spies to watch with eagle eye over the conduct of poor tenants and debtors at elections, that if they vote for the opposite party they may be sued," states the *National Aegis* in 1807.[67] "It is a fact that many mechanics are in a state of bondage in regard to electioneering suffrages,"[68] runs a New Hampshire complaint, and a few years later, "a systematic policy has for a long time guided them. No trader or mechanic friendly to government receives their custom or employment."[69] In 1810 the charge is made that throughout Massachusetts the Federalists used "blue votes" in order to recognize those who voted for Gerry.[70] Four years earlier the same practice had been introduced by the Federalists in one of the towns of Hampshire County.[71]

What was the success of Republican electioneering methods? The mere existence of a comprehensive

[66] Jefferson Papers, XLI, 2d Series, No. 52, June 2, 1805.

[67] March 25.

[68] Pol. Observatory, November 10, 1804.

[69] N. H. Gazette, April 21, 1812.

[70] Nat'l Aegis, April 4.

[71] *Ibid.*, April 16, 1806. For further comment on intimidation and undue influence, see Pol. Observatory, September 21, 1805; N. H. Gazette, September 27, 1808; Nat'l Aegis, April 11, 1810; E. Argus, November 23, 30, 1804, June 7, 1805; BENTLEY, Diary, IV, 14, 90, 92.

scheme of organization does not necessarily mean that the machine was constantly in smooth running order, but a certain degree of efficiency is undoubted.[72] As a practical result, only Connecticut remained Federalist in 1807. The severest test of Republican strength came in the following eight years and then, it is true, the Federalists retained control of the three southern states of New England and divided honors equally with their opponents in Vermont and New Hampshire. But there were other results besides those expressed by political control. The Republican propaganda had remarkable success in the first years of the century. The effect was the same all through New England, an immense increase in the total amount of voting, and from this increase the Republican party received the chief advantage. In Connecticut, as has been seen, the total voting previous to 1800 was very light. Between 1801 and 1806 the vote for governor rose from 13,413 to 22,873—a gain of approximately 70 per cent. But the Republican vote gained 792 per cent as compared with the Federalist 20 per cent. In Vermont the case is similar—gain in total vote from 10,063 to 18,682 between the years 1800 and 1807, or 85 (85.6) per cent. The Republican vote gained 205.4 per cent, the Federalist, 33 per cent. In New Hampshire the gain in the total vote is practically the same as in Connecticut, about 70 (69.3) per cent, the total vote in 1800 being 16,762, in 1805, 28,384. The Republican gain is 166.5 per cent, the Federalist 18.5 per cent. Massachusetts shows a remarkable gain in the total vote, although there is less disparity in the party gains. The total rises from 39,059 in 1800 to 81,503 in

[72] The Nat'l Aegis, January 24, 1816, at the time of reorganization of the party, contains an interesting criticism of Republican methods and charges the Boston central committee "to whom we confided this important trust" with serious dereliction of duty.

1807, approximately 106 per cent. It must be remembered, however, that the District of Maine with its growing population is included in the state. The Federalist gain is 76.8 per cent, the Republican, 146.5 per cent.

This would show that the Republican party was the popular one, that the voters who had stayed away from the polls in previous years were apt to vote the Republican ticket when they came out, and that, of the new voters, the majority probably looked on the Federalist as a decadent party and joined the Republican. In regard to this latter point the *Independent Chronicle* stated in 1807: "It is a well known fact that the rising generation is almost wholly Republican . . . and continues so until interfering interests corrupt their principles."[73] "To those who pay attention to the political state of this country," writes a Federalist, "it has been a matter of astonishment and inquiry, 'Why so many young men should have been led to imbibe the dangerous and destructive principles of Democracy?'" The writer explains the phenomenon as due to the growing irreligion and lawlessness among youths who believed that their evil propensities could be more easily gratified under Democratic rule.[74] "It is a consoling reflection that nine-tenths of our young men, farmers and mechanics who annually become voters are Republicans," says the New Hampshire *Patriot* in 1811.[75]

[73] March 30. "Reasons why Mr. Sullivan will have several thousand more votes than last year."

Ibid., November 15, 1804. "Any young man, of tolerable understanding, who has arrived at the years of action and discretion within the last ten years past, must of necessity be a Democrat. No charge of oppugnation to the Constitution can be attached to him; and however disagreeable to a person of tender understanding to be stigmatized by Scoundrels as a Jacobin; it is the part of humanity to range itself on the weakest side."

[74] Mass. Spy, April 26, 1809, Essay II. See also Salem Register, May 6, 1805.

[75] Quoted by Freeman's Press, April 11, 1811.

CHAPTER V

THE FEDERALIST REACTION, 1808-1815

Late in December, 1800, when the slowly reported results of the presidential election had at length left no doubt but that Jefferson was successful, Fisher Ames wrote to his friend, Thomas Dwight: "The weather is mild since Jefferson was elected; but it is an unwholesome and treacherous softness, that seizes the windpipe like an assassin. Storms will succeed and find us relaxed. Is not this an emblem of the smooth hypocrisy with which his reign will begin, as well as of its inevitable rigor and agitation?"[1] Outside of the natural Federalist antipathy in these words, they contained a great element of truth, and succeeding events showed that Ames was right in expecting trouble for the Republican administration. The storms which broke upon the country in 1807 and which lasted with slight intermissions for the next eight years, cost Jefferson and his party much of the prestige they had already acquired, and for a time threatened to destroy the Union. In the midst of this struggle and confusion the Federalist party recovered from the disasters of 1800-1807 and until 1815 had, on the whole, the advantage in the close and bitter political struggle which characterized the period. In 1807 Ames wrote of his party: "I declare to you, I fear Federalism will not only die, but all remembrance of it be lost. As a party, it is still good

[1] Works, II, 285.

for everything it ever was good for; that is to say, to cry 'fire' and 'stop thief' when Jacobinism attempts to burn and rob. It never had the power to put out the fire, or seize the thief."[2] Federalism still possessed enough vitality to give Republicanism a series of humiliating defeats, but it was after all a somewhat spasmodic rally, without permanent results.

The triumph of the Republicans in New England had not been marked by many revolutionary changes or proposals. In New Hampshire, when in 1804 the party first gained control of the legislature, their victory was signalized chiefly by the passage of resolutions endorsing the President, by the ratification of the twelfth amendment, and the passage of a bill creating a district system for the choice of congressional representatives, all of which measures received Governor Gilman's veto.[3] The election of Langdon in 1805 did not seem to encourage radicalism. In his message of 1806 the governor stated as subjects needing most attention, the improvement of the militia system, the establishment of a permanent seat of government, and the taking of the sense of the people in regard to a revision of the state constitution, none of which could be considered subversive of existing institutions.[4] A more serious grievance appears to have been the Republican custom of settling the succeeding day's business by a caucus the previous

[2] *Ibid.*, 391, 392. Ames to Josiah Quincy, January 27, 1807.

[3] Col. Centinel, June 20, 27, 1804. For governor's veto messages see Portsmouth Oracle, June 30.

[4] Portsmouth Oracle, June 14, 1806. N. H. Gazette, March 18, 1806. "Governor Langdon has convinced multitudes that he views all good Federalists as good Republicans. For in his numerous appointments and promotions the past year, it is very generally known that he has not been influenced in the least by sinister party or political views, but his only inquiry has been, is the candidate an honest, upright character and the friend of his country."

evening, which it was said "rendered argument in vain."[5]

In Vermont in 1807 the Republicans passed a religious liberty bill which a Federalist paper denounced as "another striking instance of the pernicious, the direful, the infernal consequences to which the leveling spirit of democracy must invariably tend. It discloses at once its great and only object, viz., the eradication of every moral, virtuous, and religious principle from the human heart."[6] Such lamentations were characteristic of Federalist publications and are probably not a fair test of public feeling.

In Massachusetts the Republican program in 1807 included a religious liberty bill, certain minor reforms in the judicial system, a law for quieting titles in Maine, and a few less important proposals.[7] The Federalists in the following spring tried to stir up alarm by claiming that the Republicans were beginning a "general war on property and religion."[8] As in 1798, however, foreign relations had the most marked effect on politics.

The old division of the people into French and British partisans had never been lost sight of. During Jefferson's first administration the Peace of Amiens, which ended, for a short time, the hostilities in Europe,

[5] Portsmouth Oracle, July 21, 1804. The Republicans seem to have introduced a similar custom into Vermont. Cf. Dartmouth Gazette, November 30, 1808. "It is said the Democratic majority in the Vermont legislature actually established a Jacobin Club under the fashionable name of caucus. . . . This continued to meet openly almost every evening for the important purpose of cutting and drying the next day's business: of devising ways and means to check the progress of federal right and federal truth. . . . The greatest precautions were used to prevent a discovery of their designs."

[6] Dartmouth Gazette, November 18, 1807.

[7] AMORY, Sullivan, II, 209, 210. An excellent account of Sullivan's administration is found, 192-215.

[8] Col. Centinel, March 23, 1808.

had apparently produced a similar effect in America. But with the reopening of the great war in 1803, the American trade with the belligerents resulted in renewed complications, which deranged public business until 1815. In 1804 Great Britain began the blockade of France and her colonial possessions. In the following year the decision in the *Essex* case made illegal the profitable "broken voyage" between the belligerent countries and their colonies. Then in 1806 and 1807 came the Decrees of Napoleon and the Orders-in-Council of Great Britain. Accompanying these difficulties was the perennial impressment grievance, which had done so much to arouse ill feeling towards the latter country. On June 22, 1807, occurred the outrage on the *Chesapeake;* in December Congress met, and on the twenty-first laid the embargo. New England had such valuable commercial interests, and people were so dependent on foreign trade, that this measure was at once brought home to practically every person in the section.[9] The political effect was soon apparent, and Jefferson's interesting experiment was disastrous to his party.

Ever since the attack on the *Chesapeake,* business had been unsatisfactory.[10] The new prohibition practically brought it to a standstill. The intense indignation which had filled the country six months earlier had now subsided, and there was nothing in such an act as the

<hr/>

[9] ADAMS, History of the United States, IV, 278-280.

[10] BENTLEY, Diary, III, 316. August 29, 1807. "We feel an almost universal stagnation of business from the late outrage on the Chesapeake. Parties are very apprehensive of war." *Ibid.*, 320. September 16. "The apprehensions of war have been great but they subside again. The public mind is much unsettled. So attached are our Seaports to bargains, that we should be hardly induced to believe that they would think of considering public liberty the best bargain."

embargo to inspire patriotism or loyalty to the administration. "The ministerialists deceive themselves egregiously if they count upon the present existence of the spirit which prevailed in July last," declared the *Columbian Centinel*.[11] And a few days later: " 'We told you so' is quite a cant phrase among the democrats. Did they tell the farmers and fishermen, that in the stagnation of business which the partial conduct of the administration was calculated to produce they would be the greatest sufferers by the hard earnings of their honest labor perishing on their hands?"[12] It was at once seen that the embargo would be the great issue in the spring elections.[13] In Massachusetts the Republicans evidently realized the seriousness of the situation. In Essex County, a delegate convention met at Ipswich on February 29, and adopted resolutions approving the conduct of the national and state administrations and endorsing the embargo "as a measure best calculated to preserve our property from plunder, our seamen from impressment, and our nation from the horrors of war."[14] Similar Republican conventions met in other counties and acted in the same way. The Federalists were equally energetic in denouncing the administration. New England was full of feverish political excite-

[11] Quoted by Portsmouth Oracle, January 2, 1808.

[12] December 30, 1807.

[13] BENTLEY, Diary, III, 337. January 5, 1808. "Politics become more sour as the severity of winter increases. Why the embargo? say all. Some reply, because of France. Some, of England. Some hope it will make the administration unpopular. Others wish to complain but they dare not give the opposition so much pleasure. Where interest prevails & patriotism is little known, we can hope nothing from the latter without some present hopes of the former. Prosperity has been at the helm & has corrupted us. Integrity cannot command, without hazard, that obedience will be refused."

[14] Ind. Chronicle, February 29, 1808. For an account of Bristol County convention, *ibid.*, March 7, Norfolk, March 21, Middlesex, March 17.

ment all through the year. County conventions, town
meetings, mass meetings, flourished as never before.[15]

In Massachusetts, Sullivan was re-elected by a greatly
reduced majority;[16] the Federalists controlled the legislature. The Republicans complained, however, that
had as many of their towns sent representatives as had
a right to do so, the result would have been different.[17]
In Connecticut the Republican vote for governor fell
off about a thousand; there was a decrease in their
strength in the legislature.[18] The New Hampshire Federalists had not recovered from the lethargy of the preceding two years, Langdon and a Republican legislature
being returned.[19] Rhode Island experienced a Federalist regeneration. In the latter state the Republican
ascendancy had been so complete that there is evidence
of a break in the dominant party. "Quiddism," which
was common in New York and Pennsylvania, appeared
only in isolated cases in New England, the even balance
of party strength keeping ranks almost unbroken. In
1805, in Rhode Island, "third parties of disappointed
office seekers" were said to have appeared in many
towns.[20] In the following year, after the death of
Arthur Fenner, there were two Republican candidates
for governor, resulting in a deadlock throughout the
year.[21] James Fenner was elected in 1807 and held
office until 1811, but in 1808 the Federalists combined
with "the moderate democrats," and, favored by the

[15] "The highest perfection of caucusing came during the embargo
period." Portsmouth Oracle, March 25, 1809.

[16] Six hundred and nineteen in a total vote of 81,147. Returns Mass.
Archives.

[17] Ind. Chronicle, May 26, 1808.

[18] Conn. Courant, April 27, 1808.

[19] Col. Centinel, June 8, 1808.

[20] Providence Phœnix, April 20, 1805.

[21] R. I. Manual, 108.

anti-embargo sentiment, elected a Federalist legislature.[22] In no state did the embargo excite deeper dissatisfaction than in Vermont, and it was not long before
the Lake Champlain region needed troops to enforce the
law.[23] As early as May it was reported that "the dying
groans of democracy echo from hill to hill in Vermont."[24] The state election did not occur until September, when Smith was defeated and Tichenor came
back to office supported by a Federalist council. The
Republicans retained control of the House.

If the change in state politics was striking, that in
national politics was no less so. Connecticut, Rhode
Island, and New Hampshire returned Federalist delegations. Vermont elected two Federalists and two
Republicans. Massachusetts, instead of eleven, now
sent only seven Republicans. In the presidential election, the latter state was unwilling to take any chances
with a popular election so the Federalist legislature
chose electors. Rhode Island and New Hampshire
chose Federalists by popular vote, Connecticut by the
legislature. In all New England, Madison received only
the vote of Vermont where the legislature, many of
whose members "were elected by a lean majority of
little boroughs many of which have not forty electors in
them and which have sent the same representation as
the largest towns in the state," chose Republicans.[25]

But while Federalism had again secured the upper
hand in New England, it had not the supremacy which
it enjoyed in the crisis of 1798. Bentley writes in his
diary while the spring election returns of Massachusetts

[22] Conn. Courant, May 11, 1808. Col. Centinel, September 7, gives result
of fall election.

[23] ADAMS, U. S., IV, 249.

[24] Col. Centinel, May 21, 1808.

[25] Ibid., November 13.

were coming in that "the great efforts have not shifted the balance but put on more weight."[26] This would perhaps not hold true of the later elections as opposition to the embargo rose steadily as the months went by, but at best Federalism had triumphed by a narrow margin only and its opponents were ready to renew the fight. Manasseh Cutler observed this and remarked in a letter to Pickering: "There is indeed considerable change, but strange as it may appear, those who continue democrats, seem to be more violent than ever. . . . It is said that Marblehead suffers more than any other town, and yet that the spirit of democracy was never higher among them. The New England democrats, I am inclined to think, are the most bitter and obstinate in the nation."[27] Furthermore, and interesting as showing the refusal of some members to remain with the party in its transition from the Federalism of Hamilton and John Adams to that of Pickering and the Hartford Convention, three prominent Federalists joined the Republican party. These were John Quincy Adams, William Plumer, and William L. Gray of Salem, the latter probably the wealthiest merchant in the United States. To join the Republicans at a time when the party was discredited, and the opposition was raging at its favorite measure, showed either a high sense of duty or the shrewdest political insight.[28]

The opposition to the embargo at length made it impossible for the administration to withstand the

[26] Diary, III, 353.

[27] Pickering MSS., XXVII, 434. Cutler to Pickering, December 28, 1808. Am. Mercury, June 2, 1809. "As the embargo is the foundation on which stands the present federal triumph, when that shall cease they will probably stand on nothing."

[28] ADAMS, U. S., IV., 240 ff.

An interesting example of successful political prophecy occurs in Am. Mercury, June 9, 1808, referring to the fact that the Federalists had won

demand for its removal. Repeal accordingly took place March 1, 1809, after a long debate in which New England Republicans joined forces with the Federalists.[29] A few days later "the late great man," as the Federalists called him,[30] departed for Monticello. Much has been written of the storm of disapproval excited by the embargo. This is undoubtedly true, but it should not be forgotten that there was always a strong Republican opposition which stood by the government.[31] Even in February, 1809, when opposition was at its height, the New Hampshire legislature sustained the Jefferson administration.[32]

The elections in four of the New England states took place while the effects of the embargo were still evident. In New Hampshire, John Langdon was defeated and the Federalists came back to power in all departments. A similar result took place in Massachusetts, where Governor Sullivan had died the preceding December, a loss which the party felt severely. The lieutenant-governor, Levi Lincoln, who succeeded him as candidate, was beaten by Christopher Gore of Boston. Rhode Island and Connecticut were Federalist, while Vermont elected Jonas Galusha, a Republican.

the Massachusetts legislature, "In the present year they can elect a federal Senator in place of Mr. Adams. What then? they will only nominate Mr. Adams to a future presidency of the United States."

PLUMER, Plumer, 365, 366. Interesting references to Gray's position in BENTLEY, Diary, III, 409-411, 414, 416.

[29] ADAMS, U. S., IV, 432-453.

[30] Col. Centinel, November 1, 1809.

[31] For accounts of town meetings which sustained the embargo, see Ind. Chronicle, August 13, 25, 29, September 1, 5, 1808; Am. Mercury, September 8, 29. There was a belief that town meetings were to a great extent inspired by the Boston Federalists. Ind. Chronicle, August 29, 1808. BENTLEY, Diary, III, 377. "The Opposition are busy in promoting measures against the embargo. These measures as usual originate in Boston. . . . Boston now originates all mischief."

[32] Portsmouth Oracle, February 18, 1809.

The fact that parties were now essentially national is shown by the fluctuation in Republican strength in New England according to the prestige gained or lost by the national administration. In 1809, in spite of the continued distress due to the losses of the previous year, and the passage of the Non-Intercourse law, there was a marked renewal of business prosperity.[33] The prospect of a settlement with England, although not ultimately realized, also served to give Madison's administration a certain temporary popularity.[34]

The revival of Republican confidence was soon apparent in the elections of 1810. Old John Langdon and his party carried New Hampshire; Galusha did the same in Vermont. In Rhode Island Fenner still held his place[35] In Massachusetts there was as usual a fiercely contested campaign. Elbridge Gerry, who had not taken a prominent part in public affairs since 1803, was brought back as Republican candidate, and his Revolutionary record invoked as an aid to the party.[36] In a total vote of more than ninety thousand Gerry received a majority, and his party had a safe margin in the legislature. Governor Treadwell of Connecticut remained "like Balaam on his Ass, determined on mischief without the power of effecting it."[37]

In the latter state Republicanism did not recover from the depression of the embargo period. In 1810 there was no Fourth of March celebration by the Republicans, and no open electioneering.[38] The long and fruitless struggle had evidently begun to discourage the

---

[33] ADAMS, U. S., V, 15-21.

[34] *Ibid.*, 66-81.

[35] Rhode Island Republican, November 7, 1810.

[36] AUSTIN, Gerry, II, 317.

[37] A Fourth of July toast to "Connecticut and Gov. Treadwell." E. Argus, July 26, 1810.

[38] Conn. Courant, April 4, 1810.

party. In this year, however, there appeared for the
first time a break in the Federalist ranks, a factional
quarrel breaking out between the friends of Treadwell
and Roger Griswold.[39] In the following year the Republicans failed to put a candidate in the field, being urged
by the *American Mercury* to support Griswold.[40] The
latter was elected, but there was no permanent fusion.
The incident is interesting as a forerunner of more
serious breaks in the dominant party which finally
brought about its downfall.

If possible, New England politics were more bitter
in the years immediately preceding the outbreak of war
than ever before. The struggle to retain control had
led to measures which were to a certain extent innovations. In 1809 Langdon was charged with turning Federalists out of office and making Republican appointments after the result of the election was known;[41] in
the year following, the Republican council was reported
to have caused the defeat of the Federalist congressional delegation by rejection of returns which had
technical defects.[42]

In Massachusetts, the constitutional right of the
towns to be represented in the General Court, according
to the number of ratable polls, led to an unseemly competition in sending representatives. The number in
the House rose from 356 in 1806 to 750 in 1812.[43] In
1810 Boston, acting on the theory that taxation and
representation went together and whereas the city paid
one eighth of the state tax it should use its constitutional right to the utmost, sent forty-two members to

[39] GREENE, Religious Liberty in Conn., 440.
[40] See March 28 for address to freemen. Also May 2.
[41] Col. Centinel, June 17, 21, 1809. Portsmouth Oracle, June 17.
[42] Col. Centinel, September 26, 29, 1810.
[43] Compiled from register in Journal.

the House.[44]   An election law regulating the qualification of town voters which was proposed by the Gore administration was considered a measure favoring Federalists,[45] and helped to bring about their defeat in 1810.

The Gerry administration, however, far surpassed any that had yet appeared in New England in the passage of partisan measures.   A public worship bill, a state bank bill, a suffrage bill were adopted.   The tenure of various state offices was changed so that the governor was able to turn out the present incumbents and substitute Republicans.   By another law, members of the legislature were to be paid from the state treasury.   The law creating new senatorial districts attracted the greatest amount of attention and made the governor's name immortal as the "gerrymander."[46]   The significance of most of these measures will be discussed elsewhere.

The importance of the District of Maine to the Republicans of Massachusetts proper was well illustrated in this administration.   Maine had a Republican majority every year from 1805 until 1815.[47]   The "Betterment Law" of 1808 was a Republican measure and greatly increased the popularity of the party among the settlers, who were now enabled to secure titles to their holdings.[48]   It was a general belief that the Republicans were inclined to favor the District while the Federalists were either indifferent or actually opposed to its interests.[49]   The Republican measures of 1810-1812 received

[44] Col. Centinel, May 16, 1810.

[45] Ind. Chronicle, February 22, 1810.   For an attack on this law as particularly injurious to the people of Maine, see E. Argus, January 18, 1810.

[46] For a concise summary of the Gerry administration see BARRY, History of Massachusetts, III, 365-368.

[47] Returns in Mass. Archives.

[48] WILLIAMSON, Maine, II, 606-608.

[49] For contrast of the Federalist and Republican attitude toward Maine, see E. Argus, May 2, 1811.

an overwhelming support from the Maine members in the legislature.[50]

The passage of the various Republican measures stirred up public feeling to a remarkable degree. The Federalists denounced them as revolutionary and criminal, while the Republicans regarded them as merely acts of justice to a large part of the population whose rights had been ignored in the past.[51] It was difficult to defend the Districting Act but Federalist precedents were discovered.[52] Combined with the local issues, the condition of foreign affairs aroused deep feeling. The attacks of French and British on American commerce served to excite the deepest resentment in both parties, each of which was active in excusing the outrages of its foreign friends. It was seen that the Massachusetts election would be a notable event, and it attracted attention throughout the country. The vote was the heaviest ever cast, and in over a hundred thousand votes Strong had a majority of about thirteen hundred. Thanks to the gerrymander the Republicans had a majority in the Senate; the House was Federalist.[53]

Coming just before the declaration of war, to which the Federalists were bitterly opposed, the loss of Massachusetts was a serious blow to the Republican party. Rhode Island had elected a Federalist governor in the previous year. The Republicans still held Vermont and

[50] On the Public Worship Bill, 84-22.
Bill Regulating Choice of Town Officers, etc., 76-20.
State Bank Bill, 35-9.
Bill Providing for payment of Members, 72-24.
House Journal, XXXII. Appendices 3, 4, 8, Sess. I; App. 3, Sess. II.

[51] See Col. Centinel, February 12, 26, March 7, 21, 25, for resolutions and other expressions of Federalist opinion. For defense of the Republicans, see Ind. Chronicle, March 19, which contains the resolution of the Central, York, and Bristol Conventions.

[52] Ind. Chronicle, March 9.

[53] BARRY, Mass., III, 369.

New Hampshire, the governor in the latter state being the ex-Federalist, William Plumer. In the presidential election Madison received only the vote of Vermont.

The struggle of the previous two years had led to determined efforts to get out the vote. In 1809 Bentley records that general caucuses seemed to have lost their reputation and "have yielded toward other subdivisions."[54] In the larger towns political societies made their appearance in 1809 and 1810. In Rhode Island the Tammany Society had flourishing lodges among the Republicans.[55] The organization of "Republican Young Men" was active in a number of places.[56]

The most interesting electioneering machine in these years, however, was of Federalist contrivance. In 1810 the Washington Benevolent Societies appeared in Rhode Island, their members being denounced as "wolves in sheep's clothing" whose real design was to break down the strength of the Tammany Society and oppose the execution of Congressional laws.[57] The organization entered Massachusetts and the neighboring states, becoming very active in 1812, particularly in Vermont and New Hampshire.[58] There were reported to be nearly a hundred of these societies in the former state in the spring of 1812.[59]

Professedly, they were for the purpose of inculcat-

[54] Diary, III, 421. "In this way conversation is personal & the disposition of the citizens is known. In general assemblies men are found from curiosity & without a knowledge of the strength of parties. In some of these private assemblies known partizans & bold intruders have been refused without ceremony. The labour has been great."

[55] See M. W. JERNEGAN, The Tammany Societies of Rhode Island.

[56] Am. Mercury, February 11, March 30, 1809.

[57] R. I. Republican, July 25, 1810.

[58] Col. Centinel, February 26, 1812, gives account of the founding and objects of the Boston society. Vt. Republican, February 10, speaks of "runners" organizing branches in various places.

[59] Ind. Chronicle, April 23.

ing patriotism and caring for indigent veterans and their dependents. Parades on Washington's birthday, or on the anniversary of the first inauguration, dinners and orations on other occasions constituted their public exercises.[60] The Republicans, however, saw a sinister purpose in these activities and were convinced that their chief object was political.[61] In an address before the society of Windsor, Vermont, an orator declared one of its objects was "to correct the political sentiments of the people."[62] In June a convention of delegates from the societies met at Woodstock to discuss plans and appoint committees for electioneering.[63] "The Washington Benevolent Societies are extending in almost every direction," declares the New Hampshire *Patriot* a year later; "they fan to a big flame the spirit of party animosity . . . and succeed in marshalling and preparing to act on all occasions, each individual of their party."[64]

The Republicans viewed the spread of the organization with great concern and showed no hesitation in freely expressing their views. A convention of Republicans at Windham, Vermont, condemned their conduct as "treason and rebellion,"[65] and a few days later the resolutions of another gathering at Woodstock declared them to be friendly to England and "dangerous by reason of their numbers, extent, and secrecy."[66] In Cheshire, Berkshire County, where the societies were

[60] Col. Centinel, May 2, 1812, gives description of a Boston celebration.

[61] Vt. Republican, March 30, 1812. Letter of S. Pond of Castleton. "Their object is not to disseminate the principles of Washington and benevolence, but to build up a party."

[62] *Ibid.*, March 2.

[63] *Ibid.*, June 8.

[64] January 12, 1813.

[65] Vt. Republican, March 9, 1812.

[66] *Ibid.*, March 16.

very strong,[67] the Republican resolutions declared "Woe to the Tories" and that the "vengeance of an indignant people" would come upon them.[68] The activity of the order seems to have subsided in 1814 but its activity is an interesting episode in New England politics during the first years of the war.[69]

The increased activity of the Federalists and the dissatisfaction aroused by the declaration of war combined to defeat the Republicans. The outbreak of war had an effect similar to that of the embargo, and as the war was of longer duration the party had no chance to recover. The most noticeable effect on the political situation was the immediate falling off in the vote, especially in southern New England. In Connecticut, politics had lost interest after 1809; in 1812 only 9747 votes were cast for governor, a decrease of 42 per cent from that of three years earlier. This was the lowest point reached by Republicanism in this state. The vote showed considerable increase in 1813, but fell to 12,721 in 1814. The Republican vote showed the worst loss. In 1812 it was 1974, in 1814, 2619. Apparently the party refused to go to the polls. The case in Rhode Island was similar. Between 1812 and 1814 the vote for governor fell from 8010 to 3542, that of the Republicans declining from 3874 to 829, a decrease of 79 per cent. The Connecticut Republicans had evidently foreseen the

[67] N. H. Patriot, May 4, 1813, estimated the membership of the county society as over 2300.

[68] Ind. Chronicle, July 27, 1812.

[69] Interesting accounts of the activity of these societies appear in N. H. Patriot, March 2, 1813. Vt. Republican, April 20, 1812. A very amusing and clever satire on this society is "The First Book of the Washington Benevolents; otherwise called the Book of the Knaves," Boston, 1813. This was followed by second, third, and fourth "books." In library of American Antiquarian Society.

See also H. H. BALLARD, "A Forgotten Fraternity." Collections Berkshire Historical and Scientific Society, III, 279-298.

decline of their party for they devised an elaborate scheme to keep up popular interest. A convention at Hartford on July 21, 1812, recommended the formation of county committees of public safety with branches in each town which by means of correspondence should encourage Republicans and keep watch on their opponents.[70] The results were rather meager, however, and in the following year the *Connecticut Courant* declared that only "the Government use of patronage and contracts" kept the party alive.[71]

In Massachusetts the Republican loss was not so marked. In the presidential election the Federalist ticket won by over twenty thousand.[72] In the next two state elections, however, the Republicans displayed much greater power. Caleb Strong was re-elected in each year, first over Joseph Varnum, then over Samuel Dexter, a prominent Federalist, who refused to accept the proposals of his party leaders and declared himself for a patriotic policy. The election returns do not indicate any sweeping changes in public sentiment. Between 1812 and 1814 the Federalist vote in Massachusetts proper gained only 2763, 6 per cent; the Republicans lost 3908, 11 per cent.[73] Maine, as will be shown, remained staunchly Republican. Unlike Connecticut and Rhode Island, there was no great decline in the total vote.[74]

In New Hampshire the amount of voting increased

[70] Am. Mercury, July 29, 1812. Similar schemes were advised in other states. See Vt. Republican, July 27; R. I. Republican, August 6, 13.

[71] April 6, 1813.

[72] Col. Centinel, December 9, 1812. The Madison ticket carried only Oxford County, Maine. Massachusetts total vote, 50,254 to 27,003.

[73] Votes in Massachusetts proper: 1812, Strong, 40,256, Gerry, 33,485; 1813, Strong, 43,019, Varnum, 27,984; 1814, Strong, 43,148, Dexter, 29,577.

[74] Total vote for Massachusetts and Maine: 1812, 104,156; 1813, 100,223; 1814, 102,477.

during the war. In 1812 Plumer had been chosen by the legislature, lacking the necessary majority because of scattering votes.[75] In 1813 he was beaten by about eight hundred, but in the following year the Federalist majority was less than one hundred. During the two years of the war the Republican candidate gained 3587 votes, the Federalist 3512; the total increase in votes was 6212.[76] A change which the Federalists made in the judicial system in 1813 was the cause of widespread dissatisfaction, and perhaps contributed to the political interest.[77] But when the decline of Republicanism in the three southern New England states is considered, the hold of the party on New Hampshire is striking, and the following boast of the Republicans seems justified, "Although we have smugglers, traitors, and abettors of the enemy in abundance, yet this little state has not been excelled by any state in the union in perseverance in correct principles, in stubborn opposition to the mountains of iniquity and corruption that have assailed its citizens on all sides."[78]

In addition to New Hampshire and Vermont, the Republicans had had their greatest strength in Maine in the years immediately preceding the war. Maine, however, unlike Vermont and New Hampshire, had a long seacoast and important commercial interests which were badly injured by the outbreak of war. But here also Republicanism held its own. In 1812 the district gave Gerry a majority of 5401; in 1813, it gave Varnum 1070; Dexter, 2655, in 1814. The falling off

---

[75] Col. Centinel, June 18, 1812. Plumer, 15,492, Gilman, 15,613, Scattering, 887.

[76] N. H. Patriot, April 5, 1814. Plumer, 19,079, Gilman, 19,125.

[77] PLUMER, Plumer, 411-414, See also N. H. Patriot, July 20, 27, August 3, 10, 17, 24, October 12, 26, November 9, 1813.

[78] N. H. Patriot, April 12, 1814.

in the vote was very slight.[79]   In the Senate, in 1814, Albion K. Parris, one of the Maine delegation, declared, "However great may be the distress of the inhabitants of Maine, he mistakes their character if he even suspects them ready to abandon the principles they have so long and uniformly supported and succumb to the tyrant of the ocean."[80]   In this year the British took possession of the country east of the Penobscot, although their actual occupation was confined to Castine and a few minor coast towns.[81]   Maine, however, did what New Hampshire and Vermont were unable to accomplish, and elected two Republican congressmen, the only ones chosen in New England.[82]

The attitude of the Republicans toward the disunion tendencies of the Federalists and especially towards the Hartford Convention, will be discussed in another connection.   Enough has been said to indicate that the Federalist ascendancy in New England during these critical years was far from complete.[83]

The history of the Republican party in New England has now been traced for a period of approximately twenty years.   Beginning with small and scattered forces the party became a great, well-organized body, which had at length gained control of all but one state in the group.   Peculiar circumstances prevented its control from being continuous, but its influence on political history of the period was of national importance.

[79] The vote of the Maine counties stood as follows: 1812, 30,407; 1813, 28,540; 1814, 30,107. Returns in Mass. Archives.

[80] E. Argus, June 16, 1814.

[81] WILLIAMSON, Maine, II, 639-648.

[82] ADAMS, U. S., VIII, 228.

[83] The Boston Patriot, January 3, 1816, quotes from the Democratic Press of Philadelphia a lengthy article advocating the election of a New England Republican to the presidency, and recounting the services of New England, military, naval, and political, during the late war.

CHAPTER VI

THE PARTY BASIS

The preceding chapters have dealt largely with the comparative strength of the Republican and Federalist parties as expressed in terms of legislative divisions or election returns, rather than with their fundamental differences in principle or membership. What were the influences which divided the population of New England into two great opposing bodies estimated in 1805 to number 580,000 of Republican and 565,000 of Federalist sympathies?[1] What appeal was made to those who voted for Elbridge Gerry or Caleb Strong, or to the eight thousand voters who kept up such a long and discouraging struggle against the Federalist régime in Connecticut? The attitude of the parties on such political questions as foreign policy or interpretation of the constitution is too well known to need comment, but this is merely indicative of more essential differences in personnel or opinion.

Edward Kendall, an Englishman who traveled through New England during the embargo period when party feeling was running high, found great difficulty in explaining to his readers the basis of the party differences which, he found, extended into the churches and even, as he expressed it, "to the graves of the dead."[2]

[1] Am. Mercury, May 23, 1805. Quoted from National Intelligencer.

[2] EDWARD AUGUSTUS KENDALL, Travels Through the Northern Parts of the United States, in the years 1807 and 1808, New York 1809, II, 131. Referring to Brewster, Mass. "Political animosities reach, too, as usual, to the church; and not only to the church, but to the graves of the dead;

The terms which he used to denote them, "Federalist" and "Anti-federalist" were rapidly becoming obsolete. For the former he found the "more modern compellations" to be "traitors, tories, damned tories, and British tories," and for the latter, "jacobins, French tories, republicans and democrats." The two last quoted terms he found hard to interpret since, from the very nature of the American system, the whole people must be at once republican and democratic. The difference of opinion he considered to be only as to the method by which the government should be administered.[3] The attitude of the parties toward the principles of the French Revolution was also an essential difference. "Democracy," he concluded, was "the name of a sect in philosophy as well as of a party in foreign and domestic politics, the sect and the party being commonly espoused by the same individual." To the Federalists "the questions of jacobinism and anti-jacobinism had appeared nearly in the same light as to the enemies of jacobinism in Europe." But more suggestive as to the real basis of party was a Federalist document which he quotes for the benefit of his readers, as "a solemn statement of the differences depending between the two."

Many people indulge an opinion, that the divisions which now agitate the public mind, originate *merely* in a difference of sentiment, respecting certain principles in politics, or the best mode of administering government. This is a sad mistake. Observe attentively the characters of those who compose a major part of the class called *democrats;* remark, likewise, the tenor of the instructions addressed to them, through

the anti-federalists want to enclose the burying ground, but the federalists are for continuing a free access to the hogs. The merits of the question do not admit of being stated with the brevity in this place required.''

3 *Ibid.*, III, 2, 3.

their public prints;—it will, then, be impossible not to see, that the controversy is of a more serious nature; that the points in dispute go to the foundation of social establishments, and aim at a total revolution in the present state of society; that ignorance, prejudice, profligacy and their concomitant, want, are marshalled and combined against all laudable eminence.

It is true, that some informed, but unprincipled men, are making use of these instruments, solely with a view to effect their own selfish plans, in pursuit of office; but should their object be accomplished, the evil will not end here. . . . That malignant hostility, which they have fostered, against those, who either by inheritance or industry, have arrived at affluence, will pursue its career, like a torrent. The line of affluence is not easily drawn; competence will be the second sacrifice. . . .[4]

This quotation is full of the characteristic pessimism of the Federalists who were continually prophesying a terrible convulsion in social and political relations[5] but nevertheless suggests an important basis for division on political questions. Property is naturally one of the first things about which people can disagree, and their attitude on the political questions concerning it is largely influenced by possession or lack of the same. The adoption of the constitution had been brought about by those whose business was suffering from the weak government of the Confederation, and opposed by those who feared what Fisher Ames styled a "debt-compelling government." The merchant whose ship was ordered back to port by the revenue officers, during the embargo, hated the Republican administration for interfering

---

[4] *Ibid.*, III, 6, 7.

[5] Cf. the following extract from a Federalist speech of 1800. "But should Jacobinism gain the ascendancy; let every man arm himself, not only to defend his property, his wife, and children, but to secure his life, from the dagger of his Jacobin neighbor." An Oration, Delivered at Deerfield on the fourth of July, 1800, by Claudius Herrick, Greenfield, Mass., 1800. Am. Ant. Soc. Library.

with his property with the same intensity as that with which the Maine squatter hated Governor Strong, whom he held responsible for his own eviction and the confiscation of his improvements. The effect of the land tax in 1799 has already been discussed.

Contemporary opinion tended to look at party divisions as the result of commercial, that is, property questions. "I apply without hesitation," writes one Federalist in explaining the rise of party spirit in 1793, "the term Rabble to that numerous class of degenerate mankind who are destitute of honor, character, and property and are the accustomed tools of every inflammatory demagogue. There are such among every people, no matter how they may be dignified by the French and Bostonians with the honorable title of citizen."[6] Says another, "Society consists of two classes; of those who have something and want to keep it, and of the rabble who have got nothing and are ever ready to be stirred up to get everything."[7] The Republican view was similar, but of course from the standpoint of the righteous opponents of the overwhelming power of wealth. "Aristocracy has sprung up through the means of unusual and overgrown wealth created by the funding system without industry," declared the *Independent Chronicle* in the course of its campaign against Fisher Ames in 1794.[8] "The great conflict between the Federal and Republican parties in this country originated principally in the different views and motives which actuated the commercial and landed interests. . . . Commerce accumulates great wealth in the hands of individuals. . . . Farmers wish for a government simple and frugal in its administration."

[6] Conn. Courant, February 11, 1793.
[7] Col. Centinel, January 31, 1801.
[8] September 2, 1794.

Whether this is the true explanation for the origin of the party division or not, there is abundant evidence that the Republican movement was that of the non-property holding classes. The nature of electioneering appeals bears out the charge which Kendall quoted. They are full of assaults on the merchants, the banks and other corporations, and the defenders of property interests, the courts and lawyers. The same tendency is seen in the Republican demand for the abolition of property qualifications for suffrage, and in such local questions as the election law in Connecticut, or the disfranchisement of plantations in Massachusetts. The Federalists are equally vigorous in the defense of these interests.

The hostility toward the mercantile interest is apparent even before party lines were clearly drawn. An address to the people by William Lithgow, a candidate for Congress in the Lincoln district of Maine in 1791, gives an elaborate denial of an opponent's charge that he is "in favor of the mercantile as opposed to the landed interest" or that he is opposed to "laying duties on superfluities entering the United States." It has uniformly been his opinion that the land tax ought never to be resorted to by Congress except in cases of great emergency. There should be no hindrances to agriculture, "that energetic and primary support of our national government."[9] The Republican opposition to the funding system and establishment of the national bank needs no comment; their influence in solidifying the party is well known. The same attitude is taken towards the Jay Treaty, and the Federalists considered it a "remarkable and undeniable fact" that the most violent clamors about losses at sea and about the treaty, came from those who "had lost nothing and had noth-

9 Col. Centinel, May 11, 1791.

ing to lose.''[10] The navy was objected to as an institution for which people had to pay while its effect was to make the merchants a privileged order. The protection of the carrying trade was intended to aggrandize a few. ''To the farmer it is of no importance who carries his produce abroad, or who brings his merchandize.''[11] The dependence of all classes in New England on commercial prosperity was not properly realized until the embargo was laid. The commercial policy of the Republicans was of course the argument chiefly used by the New England Federalists in justifying their stubborn opposition. On such questions as the embargo or the declaration of war the clash of interests is always apparent.[12] The ''English influence'' under which the Federalists were supposed to be, was merely a feature of the same feeling. Kendall noted the dependence of large numbers on the credit given by the village store, which in turn was indebted to the merchant in the seaports, who had imported his goods on credit allowed by the English exporter.[13]

[10] U. S. Chronicle, July 30, 1795. The Ind. Chronicle, October 15, 1795, mentions the fact that General Knox had entertained over four hundred of his fellow citizens and that principle had been sacrificed to eating and drinking. ''The citizens who are opposed to the treaty are not able to give entertainment at their 'seats.' ''

[11] Am. Mercury, August 20, September 17, 1807. ''Politics for Connecticut Farmers.''

[12] The following is typical of the despairing tone of the Federalist press. This is part of a comment on the President's message, December, 1812. ''By this message, the last ray of hope for peace is extinguished. . . . The merchants' eye must cease to linger on the ocean and the gilded clouds which bound his horizon. He must learn to consider the glaciers of Canada as more splendid objects of contemplation and to console himself that the wreck of his fortunes may yet enable him to establish his children among 'God's chosen people' in the back regions of Virginia, Kentucky, or Ohio.''

[13] Travels, III, 289. Cf. Freeman's Press (Montpelier, Vt.), September 8, 1809. ''The town of Boston controls the internal commerce of New

In no state is the hostility toward the mercantile interest plainer than in Rhode Island. The long and bitter struggle over the adoption of the constitution had been between the rural classes and the commercial interests of Providence.[14] Arthur Fenner had been the candidate of the anti-commercial faction in 1791,[15] but this did not cease to be a merit. In 1803 an address on his behalf reads: "The high toned Federalists are those who were in a prosperous condition at the close of the Revolution. . . . Fenner defended the cause of the farmers at this time, and helped to shift the burden on covetous and unrighteous speculators. He has always been hated by the merchant class."[16] Again, he had rescued "the oppressed farmers of 1786 from the hands of a merciless crowd of creditors. . . . There are always two parties, merchants and speculators, honest farmers and citizens."[17] In 1811 there is a savage Republican attack on the Federalist senatorial ticket which contained the names of seven merchants, and had been made out in Providence to enable that city to rule the state.[18] The Federalists deprecated the raising of issues between the farmers and merchants.[19]

The commercial centers were, with the exception of Portsmouth and Salem, strongly Federalist. New Haven and Providence were not once carried by the Republicans between 1800 and 1815. Newport was Fed-

England. . . . Every country trader is indebted to the merchants of Boston and the people of the interior to the country trader."

[14] BATES, R. I. and Formation of Union, 167, 170-172.

[15] *Ibid.*, 184.

[16] Providence Phœnix, May 28, 1803.

[17] *Ibid.*, June 4.

[18] R. I. Republican, April 20. Cf. *ibid.*, October 25, 1809. "The merchant has the advantage over part of the community whose poverty makes them dependent on him. He trifles with their right of suffrage."

[19] R. I. American, April 5, 1811.

eralist after 1805.[20]   Boston voted for Gerry in 1800,
but the Federalists were successful in every other year.
Portland was carried by the Republicans only once—
in 1811.[21]   Boston, as the commercial center of New
England and the headquarters of the leading Federalists, was always an object of intense dislike to the
Republicans. "Freedom of election in the metropolis
is a mere shadow," says one writer. "The influence
of monied Associations, purse proud merchants, and
prattling lawyers is such that Mechanics and Laborers
do not and cannot express their opinions even by the
secrecy of the ballot."[22]   The dislike was especially
strong in the District of Maine. "Will not some able
pens be employed in freeing us from a dependence on a
distant territory, whose capital seems devoted to corruption, degredation and ruin?"[23]

The banking business was looked on with great suspicion by many and the Republican press is filled with
attacks on such institutions as engines of Federalist
oppression. The importance of the banking question in

[20] From examination of newspaper reports of elections.

[21] Returns in Mass. Archives.

[22] E. Argus, March 2, 1805. *Ibid.*, May 17. "As the leading opposi-
tionists are leaving their respective counties and thronging to Boston, in
order to become presidents of Banks and Insurance Companies . . . it
will be well to drop the appellation of Essex Junto hereafter and call these
movers of high handed measures the Boston Junto." In 1799 the Ind.
Chronicle, April 8, accounted for the Federalism of Boston by explaining
that "National Bank Connections, enemies of the Revolution, little British
agents, great British residents, ship building interests and the military,
form a phalanx which overpowers the free and independent citizens." See
also November 22, 1804.

[23] E. Argus, June 7, 1804.

Cf. ABRAHAM BISHOP, Wallingford Oration, 20. There was no support
for Republicanism in great cities. "In all our commercial towns aristocracy was forming like a mighty cancer and its fibres were extending
into all the interior country. Wherever these extended, republicanism
suffered. The corn merchant, the grazier, the rich farmer were all crying
out, 'We have a blessed government, we are all becoming rich.'"

New Hampshire, where it caused the formation of the first organized opposition to the Gilman administration is merely an indication of the belief that Federalism, the party of wealth, was determined to reduce competition to a minimum. "It is well known throughout the United States," says a Republican history of this affair, "what use was made of incorporated banks from 1795 to 1800—that persons called republicans could obtain little or no accommodation from them—that they were used as a powerful instrument to awe the minds of men, and make them act in conformity to the politics of wealthy owners of capital."[24]

The sinister influence which the bank exerted on the voter was a favorite subject of complaint with Republicans; the influence of the Boston banks has already been mentioned. "The lawyers incorporate banks, whose influence over votes is great beyond calculation," runs a Connecticut complaint.[25] In Massachusetts the Republican hostility led to a demand for greater control over such institutions by the state—which the Federalists considered "an attempt to enlist the banking subject to aid the depreciating cause of democracy."[26] In Maine this demand was put forward in a series of papers published in the *Eastern Argus* in 1805. The writer, who claims to voice the sentiments of a Republican, complains of the fact that the legislature spends most of its time granting charters to banks and turnpike companies. The purpose of incorporations was to give exclusive privileges to Federal friends and "every incorporation for wealth and profit is a bulwark to aristocracy." The increase of corporations tends "to sink the individual out of notice and he loses his equal

24 N. H. Gazette, February 26, 1805.
25 Am. Mercury, February 27, 1806.
26 Col. Centinel, September 6, 1809. See also June 21, 1806.

protection."[27] Most of the banking corporations would
expire in 1812 and "incorporations should not be
renewed unless the proprietors of banks consent that
every officer of their banks be appointed by the State
Government."[28] A year later an address to the Republicans urges them to send their full quota of representatives in order to prevent the coming of the time when
would be seen "your rivers blocked up with toll bridges
and your farms cut into inch pieces by Turnpike roads,
and your every privilege taken away by incorporated
Federalism."[29] The banking question played an important part in the election of the Gerry administration in
1811 and there the Republican doctrine is again evident.
"The Republicans believe that in renewing the charters of the banks the state shall receive a proportion of
the profits; the Federalists say they have all the money
and that they will continue to conduct the banking business for their own benefit if the Federal towns will only
follow the example of Boston and send more representatives."[30] The chartering of the so-called State Bank
by this administration was a distinctly Republican
measure and was the subject of bitter criticism by the
Federalists.[31]

[27] E. Argus, November 15, 1805.

[28] *Ibid.*, December 13. See also November 8, 22, 29, December 6.

[29] *Ibid.*, May 2, 1806.

Cf. Resolutions of town of Tisbury, 1810. "Whereas the Legislature has
incorporated banks for the exclusive benefit of a few and allowed them to
circulate small notes, while forbidding private individuals passing theirs
. . . we view this as subversive of the bill of rights. . . . We consider
that no incorporation of men have any title to obtain privileges distinct
from ordinary individuals. . . . We view the banking system in all its
parts as destructive of moral principles." Quoted by E. Argus, January
4, 1810.

[30] E. Argus, May 2, 1811. James Sullivan advocated that the state
receive a share in the banking business in a pamphlet which was published
after his death. The Path to Riches, Boston, 1809.

[31] "The state has a right at any time to be interested to the amount

The same Republican hostility to moneyed interests is apparent in Vermont. "Their tendency," says one writer in discussing the advisability of chartering banks, "will be to facilitate the unequal distribution of property as will eventually eradicate from our country, the very principles of republicanism. . . . I have long regarded the banking system as a federal project."[32] "Middling class farmers cannot obtain money at banks," says another.[33] Until 1806 Vermont was without a bank, but in this year a prominent Republican, Titus Hutchinson, secured the passage of a bill establishing the Vermont State Bank, a purely governmental institution, its directors state employees, and revenues of the state pledged in place of capital stock.[34]

But the fact that the Republicans were the party of the poorer classes does not appear alone in their hostility to banks and corporations. There is direct testimony on the membership of the parties. Uriah Tracy, writing to Oliver Wolcott and describing the result of the spring election in Litchfield, remarked: "Kirby is, to

of one-third of the stock and to appoint one-third of the directors and the state receives a handsome revenue by way of tax from the bank. . . . It is the first bank required to pay a tax to the state. . . . The other banks will be subject to this, hence the Federal hostility." Article on the State Bank, Ind. Chronicle, August 26, 1811. *Ibid.*, April 6, 1812. "It [the bank] is opposed to the great monied aristocracy which has monopolized all banking advantages for many years."

32 Spooner's Vt. Journal, March 6, 1804.

33 Pol. Observatory, January 21, 1804. See series of articles on banks quoted from Spooner's Vt. Journal, December 24, 31, 1803, January 7, 14, 21, 1804.

34 For an interesting history of this institution see H. S. DANA, History of Woodstock, Vt., Boston, 1889, 332 ff. "The anti-bankites averred that all corporations were opposed to republican principles, being the foundations or the relics of monarchy, and none more so than banks and turnpikes; that a money corporation would produce a moneyed influence and this influence would be excited in particular to corrupt elections." Also Records of Governor and Council, V, 443-451.

the disgrace of this town again chosen deputy, but he has no cause of triumph. I am mistaken if his defeat is not written in legible characters on this day's proceedings; all the solid, respectable part of the town without any preconcert or intrigue voted against him, and the third time going around, he just obtained, by the aid of every rag tag who could be mustered, and a whole winter of intrigue and very expensive intrigue too. . . . ."[35] Bentley, enthusiastic Republican though he was, admitted that at the election of 1796 "the men of property appeared chiefly for Sumner" and that "the democratic party were not without men of firm minds, but were not qualified by education to plead or write."[36] The opinion of the party about its own membership may be worth quoting. In 1807 when the Republicans had elected their first governor in Massachusetts, the Philadelphia *Aurora* described it as "a contest between the people, the farmers, mechanics, and tradesmen on one side, and the 'natural aristocracy of the land,' the well-born, the best blood of the country, the men above the dull pursuits of civil life on the other side."[37] "The hardy Yeomanry, the tradesmen and the body of militia are the Republican phalanx," says another account.[38]

The intolerable insolence of the Federalists toward their opponents is a striking characteristic of the con-

[35] GIBBS, Memoirs, II, 232.   Tracy to Wolcott, April 8, 1799.

[36] Diary, II, 176. *Ibid.*, III, 77. Referring to a Republican caucus on March 10, 1804. "They appear to have union & strength. They need talents, but as they have few public speakers they do their business more coolly & in a shorter time." Cf. Plumer's comment on the Portsmouth opposition in a letter to Jeremiah Smith, October 17, 1795. "The latter, as to numbers are the most numerous, tho far from being so as it respects talents, integrity, & all that is valuable in man." MSS., I, 260.

[37] Quoted by Ind. Chronicle, June 8, 1807.

[38] *Ibid.*, April 17, 1809.

test, and, in a way, throws considerable light on the real party division. A typical description of the New England Democrats occurs in the *Connecticut Courant* of April 6, 1803.

Their principal leaders are men desperate in fortunes as in morals. Adultery, dissipation and debauchery had marked several of them among the outcasts of mankind. . . . A few who have acquired wealth and wish to gain office and who have been promised promotion . . . some who have been disappointed in ambition . . . a few honest men who have been the dupes of Jacobin falsehood. The residue is of the dregs of mankind. Aliens who have fortunately fled from the whipping post and gallows in their own country, and the rabble of our own, the slaves of vice and indigence, men easily led by demagogues.

Two years earlier the same paper had described the party as composed of

a class of people always peevish and uneasy. . . . This faction comprehends all the loose and infamous and desperate portions of society . . . the sons of Belial and lewd fellows of the baser sort.[39]

A Massachusetts picture is similar:

The leaders of our Eastern Democracy are quite a distinct order of men. They are rarely distinguished by education, talents, or any description of pre-eminent worth. Their electors do not compose the most respectable or substantial classes in society, though among them are to be found many men entitled to that character. They are strong at perceiving distinctions which are quite independent of universal suffrage. Fraught with the jealousies and antipathies of vulgar minds they are prone to suspicion. These men can never be reformed by good example or good company. Their quarrel is with nature and is eternal.[40]

[39] February 2, 1801.

[40] Col. Centinel, March 28, 1812. The following anecdote which goes the round of the Republican press in 1804, illustrates the same point. A

Such descriptions cannot be taken literally any more than the Republican description of Sumner's supporters in 1797, "old Tories and men strongly attached to monarchy and aristocracy."[41] Their significance is in showing a decided tendency to draw party lines according to social or class lines. The Federalist contempt for the opposing party is that of the educated, prosperous, and conservative possessor of political power, who sees the encroachments of a different order of people which he has regarded as not entitled to a share in such privileges. The Republican attitude is that of the determined opponent of privilege who claims and fights for political recognition. The Republicans were the poorer part of the population; their opponents, the men of property, the leading families, the lawyers, the clergy, were obnoxious as the holders of a monopoly of political power. As has been seen in a previous chapter the great feature of the Republican movement was the increase in political interest among the mass of the people. The huge accessions to the Republican party between 1800 and 1815 lead to the conclusion that previous Federalist predominance was due to the absence of an energetic opposition, and the success of the Republicans came by getting into action the potential strength of a great mass of voters hitherto quiescent or indifferent. The spur used was distinctly an appeal to class jealousy. Hence the Republican movement in

Federalist and Republican meet and discuss the rapid increase of Republicanism in New England. "But how happens it," says the Federalist, "that the converts you make to democracy are all of the low, ragamuffin sort of people, who can do no honor to your cause?" "Why, for a very good reason, we have nothing but federalists to make them out of." Spooner's Vt. Journal, April 3, 1804.

The Col. Centinel, January 14, 1801, gives in parallel columns the names of prominent Federalists and Republicans in various professions and invites the people to compare their character and general standing.

41 Ind. Chronicle, February 2, 1797.

New England has a character fortunately unusual in American politics. It was not altogether a struggle for principle; the politician is always in evidence with his selfish projects,[42] but to the success of this movement is probably due the breaking down of class lines in subsequent parties.

Deep distrust of government by the people was characteristic of the Federalist.[43] The utterances of the leading members of the party on this subject are well known. Republicanism stood for confidence in the ability of the people as a whole to manage their affairs. While Fisher Ames wrote, "Democracy is a troubled spirit, fated never to rest, and whose dreams, if it sleeps, present only visions of hell,"[44] his brother declares, "Whoever attempts to introduce a government beyond the complete control of the whole people is accessory to treason against all the rest of mankind! And if he succeeds he is a Traitor!"[45]

[42] Kendall noted the cynical contempt of the politician for the "sovereign people," except when electioneering. "In public men talk to you of the wisdom and large information of the American people;—you wink at the imposture, and restrain your laughter;—they thank you for the complaisance, and presently whisper in your ear—that *the people know no more than horses*. In Massachusetts, an established idol of the people, and one who had therefore talked much to the people of their wisdom and their virtue, made to myself these serious assertions: That there is not a spark of public virtue in all the whole commonwealth, and that the members of the legislature assemble only for purposes of private gain," etc. Travels, III, 228. See also 265-266.

[43] Cf. the following: " 'Vox populi, vox Dei' is an apothegm, that has gone hand in hand with destruction. . . . Yet this is the wandering star, which rules and guides the destiny of our nation. The people are an ocean, that ever ebbs and flows; easily moved by every breath which curls upon the surface. The two great engines, by which they may always be agitated are the thirst for riches and the dread of domination." An Oration pronounced at Northampton, July 4, 1805, by Isaac C. Bates. Northampton, 1805. Am. Ant. Soc. Library.

[44] Works, I, 337.

[45] Diary, April 11, 1806. Cf. Providence Phœnix, June 22, 1802.

The Federalist party had its chief strength, as has been mentioned, in the people of property, the lawyers and educated classes, and the clergy. The clergy and the religious question in general in this period form a subject of such importance as to need a separate consideration. The Republicans recognized this union among their opponents. "Lawyers, merchants, and clergymen are laboring in support of patriotic principles," says a sarcastic writer in Rhode Island.[46] "In Connecticut, Federalism is strongly fortified. It has secured in its interests the college, the clergy, the bar, the monied institutions, the religious and literary societies and most of the presses. It has complete annual control over the military and judiciary department."[47] The same seems to be true of the other states.[48] "The Federalists in this state have long considered the possession of office as a vested right," remarks one Massachusetts orator.[49]

The rousing of popular feeling against the dominance of this régime was the work of the Republicans and the

"Republican Creed" by "Leather Breeches Weaver." "1. The people have a right to adopt their own form of government. 2. To appoint their own rulers. . . . 3. Never do anything in government that will impair the rights of a portion of the citizens, for the express purpose of aggrandizing others, lest it open a door for tyrrany to walk in at."

[46] R. I. Republican, October 25, 1809. "Patriot."

[47] Am. Mercury, August 29, 1806. In regard to Federalist influence on the press, note Ames' description of the Dedham paper, "wholly dictated by F. A. to smother political enquiry and make public servants Lords." Diary, October 11, 1796.

[48] STORY, Life and Works of Joseph Story, 96. "The preponderance of wealth, rank, talent, and civil and literary character of the state were with the Federalists." The Vt. Republican, February 13, 1809, states that in Windsor County there were seventeen Federal lawyers, and five Republican, twenty-four Federal merchants and nine Republican. These were "leaders in electioneering" for the Federalists.

[49] An Oration Pronounced at Charlestown, Mass., July 4, 1811. Anon. Am. Ant. Soc. Library.

invoking of social prejudice is constantly evident.
"They are to govern, you are to be governed. They
are well born, you are base born," was the burden of Abraham Bishop's invective against the Connecticut "aristocrats."[50]   In 1798 an address to the Connecticut voters warns them that there are two classes
of people, the mechanics and farmers, who produce
goods for the community, and others "living by cun-
ning"—merchants, speculators, priests, lawyers, and
government employees. "Particularly in New England
we have confided government too much to this class of
citizens." "Why are things so managed that there are
not ordinarily more than 1600 votes given for a member
of Congress in Connecticut? . . . They dread your
uncorrupted hearts; in them they yet behold the awful
image of republicanism. They wish to avoid election,
they choose representatives from the state at large so
you may not know for whom you vote and not be interested enough to attend elections. . . . Is it not mock-
ery, to call that a government of the people?"[51] "How
often," says a Republican orator, "are sentiments
advanced which disgrace the American name—'the
common people have nothing to do with politics; there
are men who are bred to the business.' How often do
they observe 'that such a man is a mechanic or a common laborer—how should he know about these matters;
it takes a great deal of hard study and learning to make
a lawyer, and in addition to these a vast deal more to
qualify a man for a politician. These men therefore had
better attend to the plow and hoe.' "[52]

[50] Origin and Progress of Political Delusion, 29.

[51] Ind. Chronicle, April 13, 1798.   Quoted from Middlesex Gazette.

[52] Republicanism and Aristocracy contrasted; or, the Steady Habits
of Connecticut inconsistent with and opposed to the Principles of the
American Revolution, exhibited in an Oration delivered at New London,

The same appeal to social feeling is evident in such an address as the following:

Has not the legislative majority of judges and justices provided by law that the poor man who trudged on foot his weary pilgrimage through life should do the same quantity of labor on the public roads as the rich man; while the justice, or judge, the Clergyman and Physician who encumbered the highways with his wagons, six cattle team and pleasure carriage should have no part of the burthen? . . . They possess more than the average amount of property to defend. Where will you find a law by which your law making justices have enrolled themselves in the militia? . . . Rulers become jealous of their subjects; enquiry is branded with the opprobious term of licentiousness, reform is styled innovation, the desire of civil liberty enmity to order, and the love of religious liberty is stigmatized with the name of infidelity.[53]

The Republicans directed their attack against those local leaders who had apparently possessed political control in many towns. Abraham Bishop assailed as one of the serious obstacles in the way of Republican success "the family alliances, producing patriarchs in opinion and the too general habit of whole towns committing to a few individuals the power to dictate to them opinions on all subjects. . . . The houses of York

Conn., July 4, 1804, by Christopher Manwaring. Norwich, Conn., 1804. Am. Ant. Soc. Library.

Cf. Am. Mercury, March 26, 1807. "There was a time in this country when God had created all men equal and had given to each man certain unalienable rights; but the new creation of federalism has thrown into confusion the first creation. . . . It has created four or five hundred gentlemen having entire right to rule and reign."

[53] Am. Mercury, April 3, 1802. "Hancock."

The Federalists deeply resented the Republican uprising. A reply to Bishop's oration on Political Delusion carries this motto, "Likewise these filthy dreamers despise dominion and speak evil of dignities." Three Letters to Abraham Bishop, Esq., by Connecticutensis, New Haven, 1800.

and Lancaster are united in most of our towns."[54]
"The political faith and practice of each country town
depend in a great measure on that of three characters,"
says a writer in the *Eastern Argus*. These were the
minister, the lawyer, and physician. The first two professions were almost entirely monopolized by the Federalists; the writer of the above asserts that the doctors
were generally "the friends of freemen."[55] A Connecticut writer on the contrary states that "since federalism took up its abode in our happy state, the Clergy,
Physicians and the Lawyers have united harmoniously
together, a band of pious brethren and true Christians."[56] The use of printed nomination lists was
defended by the Republicans on the ground that under
the existing system nominations in freemen's meeting
were made by one or two persons and "the personal
influence of the nominator" was often an overwhelming
influence. In some towns it was said, "at the call of
each name a significant wink, nod, or shake of the head
is made by some dictator of the meeting."[57] A Republican sketch of a Federalist caucus puts the following
words in the mouth of a speaker: "Mr. President, I

[54] Wallingford Oration, March 4, 1801, p. 17. Cf. Ames' Diary, December 30, 1802: "The parish, that is F. Ames and Dr. Bullard." . . .

[55] E. Argus, December 2, 1803. A number of prominent Massachusetts
Republicans were physicians, Jarvis, Eustis, Kittredge, Nathaniel Ames,
Kilham.

Nathaniel Ames in his diary, November 4, 1796, writes, "The Prigarchy
straining every nerve to carry election." Was the "Prigarchy" this local
clique?

[56] Am. Mercury, June 20, 1805. Cf. Gideon Granger to Jefferson,
October 18, 1800, stating that there were "at least four hundred men of
public education and prospects for four or five of us to contend with. . . .
I have long labored to rally the Physicians & Dissenting Clergy who are
generally friends of equal liberty." Jefferson Papers, 2d Series, XXXVI,
No. 27.

[57] Am. Mercury, September 11, 1800.

have very particular reasons against the dissemination of Republican principles in my town, where I now exercise a sort of aristocratic sway. An English nobleman cannot have greater influence in his borough than I have in our town meetings. I direct the people for whom and for what to vote on all occasions."[58]

The Connecticut Election Law of 1801 has been referred to in another connection. One clause in the act required the voter to stand up when stating his vote, hence the law was generally known as the "Stand-up Law." The fact that this was a Federalist measure and the character of the protests against it show the essential difference in the parties and the nature of the struggle. The Republican minority at the passage of the law had filed a protest which states that "under the old law every freeman could vote by ballot in secret. Undue influence of authority and office, of hard and tyrannical creditors, of oppressive landlords, of prevalence of public sentiment, and the chords of affection or connection derived from friendship, blood or union in business was prevented and checked. By the present law these are brought into operation."[59]

The lawyer was always under Republican disfavor. Kendall noted the alliance between the storekeeper and the lawyer.[60] The latter made a decent living by collecting the debts due the former, the fees on small amounts being always high. The lawyer usually combined politics with his other business and in very many instances represented the town in the legislature, constituting what Dr. Ames styled the "pettifogging inter-

[58] Nat'l Aegis, October 3, 1804.

[59] This minority protest appears in full in Am. Mercury, November 5, 1801. An attempt was made to repeal this law in 1808. The debate on the proposed repeal appearing in Am. Mercury, June 9.

[60] Travels, III, 34.

est.''[61] None of the "privileged orders" were sub-
jected to more savage attack. "A lawyer in every
man's mess here, nothing will go with Fools without a
Lawyer, but from good company they are excluded! or
if they get in they spoil it," writes Ames.[62] But the
distrust of the lawyers was more than personal prejudice. The fact that they constituted a strong faction
in legislatures was believed to be an interference with
the separation of powers. "Will we not see—will not
the people yet be convinced that their all, their salva-
tion depends on a frequent change of legislatures going
fresh with the feelings of the people to make the laws,
not as intriguers to bit and gag them, then to mount and
ride them. The making Lawyers legislators seems to
defeat the grand principle of keeping the legislative
department separate from the Judiciary and where
these two or any two of the three departments of Government are confided to the same hands, though the
forms under the real sovereignty of the people are preserved to amuse them the substance is gone.''[63]

The fact that a majority of the Federal candidates for
office were lawyers furnished campaign arguments for
their opponents. In 1795 the voters were urged to
defeat Samuel Dexter, one of the leading members of
the Massachusetts bar, and representative of the Middlesex district. Nine lawyers from one state were said
to be sufficient; his opponent, Joseph Varnum, was a
farmer and there had "never been a real farmer in
Congress from this state.''[64] The defeat of Dexter was

[61] Diary, February 28, 1806.
Cf. *ibid.*, April 3, 1803. ''Washington, dupe of the Order of Lawyers
while he was alive renounced them after he was dead—I will not do so. I
will renounce them now I am alive and leave them to their luck after.''
[62] *Ibid.*, April 3, 1802.
[63] *Ibid.*, February 8, 1799.
[64] Ind. Chronicle, March 19, 1795.

one of the first important Republican victories in Massachusetts. In spite of Republican opposition to the merchants, the latter was preferable to the lawyer. In Maine, in 1810, three Republican candidates for Congress, Cutts, Widgery, and Tallman, were held up to the voters as the "commercial and agricultural ticket opposed to aristocratic lawyers."[65] "Do you wish to avoid the barbarous principles of the laws of England, and have a Lord Bacon or a Camden who lived a hundred years ago decide your case by precedents having no relation to your cause? . . . Do you wish to avoid an additional list of attorneys, pettifoggers and litigators? . . . then vote for the Farmer's Republican Ticket."[66] This is the language of a Vermont address. In New Hampshire the Federalist ticket in 1814—styled by themselves the "American Peace Ticket"—is called "five sharks of the green bag."[67] Among the names of the "sharks" appears that of Daniel Webster. In Connecticut the feeling against the lawyers was particularly bitter. Bishop inveighed against them,[68] and hardly a number of the *American Mercury* is free from attacks similar to the above.

There were not many Republican lawyers, but the party, especially in Massachusetts, was taunted with inconsistency in supporting such men as James Sullivan or Levi Lincoln.[69] There were misgivings, however, among Republicans for having to do so, and after Sulli-

[65] E. Argus, October 25, November 1.

[66] Green Mountain Farmer (Bennington), September 4, 1809.

[67] N. H. Patriot, July 19, 1814.

[68] Political Delusion, 83.

[69] Portsmouth Oracle, April 18, 1807. "Next to our Connecticut patriots, the antifederalists of Massachusetts are supposed to be the most implacable foes of lawyers which New England can produce." The writer then remarks that the Republican candidate for governor and leaders in the legislature were lawyers.

van's death Bentley writes, "Nothing was objected to him seriously, but what belonged to his habits as a lawyer, & of this character the people are the most jealous as it is the only one to which the people of this country generally attribute habitual dishonesty."[70]

The distrust of the lawyers extended also to the courts. Judge Chase was not the only judge who was believed to be using the bench for political purposes. The courts in the New England states at this time were not well organized and there are continual complaints in the press about the delay and expense of litigation.[71] But these were minor grievances compared with the belief that the judges were influenced by party feeling. Judge Dana of Massachusetts was accused in 1796 of censuring in a charge to the Plymouth grand jury all opponents of the Federal administration and stigmatizing Republican papers as "organs of calumny and sedition," and in other addresses was said to have reprobated the Democratic societies.[72] An article addressed to the Supreme Court of the same state in 1803 warns them: "No Republican has a seat on your bench or is admitted to a participation in your judicial consultations. . . . Notwithstanding the boasted independence of the Judiciary you are not exalted above responsibility but are answerable at least at the bar of public opinion."[73] The distrust and dislike for the courts was apparent in the opposition to increasing the salaries of the judges. "While Young Adams is working into

[70] Diary, III, 401.

[71] Ind. Chronicle, November 2, 1809, states that complaint is general throughout New England. "The laws are made by the whole people and the expenses are paid by them. It is therefore a hard case that they should become the sole property of the lawyers to be sold to the people at whatever extravagant price they may see proper to put upon them."

[72] *Ibid.*, June 2, 1796.

[73] Ind. Chronicle, February 14, 1803. "Amicus Curiæ."

political favor," writes Bentley in 1808, "young Story of the Law in this town is working out. As soon as he reached as far as the public favor could carry him, the House of Representatives—he fell into the hands of the opposition & dared to come forward with a project of salaries for the Judges which the opposition could not in the days of their glory obtain. . . . He dared still to venture & the next time came with three bills of Judicature."[74]

In Connecticut the appointment of the judges by the legislature where there was always a Federal majority led to charges of party influence and unfairness.[75] In the other states there is less evidence of feeling against the judges, although Vermont in 1808 approved an amendment making United States judges removable on address by Congress.[76] The reorganization of the New Hampshire courts in 1814 by a Federalist legislature created considerable excitement for a short time but the changes remained permanent.[77]

But the most interesting and characteristic feature of this part of the Republican movement is the demand for greater responsibility to the people, and this after all is its most important phase. The following is a typical expression of this feeling:

The independence and infallibility of the judiciary, is now the last recourse and stronghold of Tory federalism . . . the people are called upon to determine whether or how long they are to submit to the disposition of an independent judiciary

[74] Diary, III, 346. Cf. MORISON, Jeremiah Smith, 247-248. Smith's unpopularity was due in part to his recommending an increase in judges' salaries.

[75] Am. Mercury, February 27, 1806. "Judges and justices are glorious retailers of the will of their makers. They serve as committees to drag up voters."

[76] Records of Governor and Council, V, 418, 419.

[77] MORISON, Jeremiah Smith, 265-277. PLUMER, Plumer, 412-414.

in the hands of the Federalists, combined with the shameful uncertainty of the law.[78]

And again:

The Federalists call the attempt to reform the Judiciary disorganizing . . . to render the Judges responsible, agreeable to the constitution, is styled ''hunting the Judges.'' Anything relating to the judiciary is considered by the federalists as trespassing on sacred ground, as if judges and lawyers were possessed of as much infallibility as the pope and the Catholic hierarchy. Within the United States there is as much pains taken to render the judges independent of every control as in Spain and Algiers to make His Holiness and Mohammet superior to every check from their ignorant proselytes.[79]

Another interesting demand appears at this time, that judges should be elective.[80] John Leland of Berkshire, one of the most interesting of the New England Republicans, although he was notable chiefly as a leader in the movement for religious liberty, laid down the principles of this doctrine in 1805.

[78] Ind. Chronicle, February 22, 1808.

[79] *Ibid.*, February 18, 1808. Cf. BENTLEY, Diary, III, 387. ''The truth is the Gentlemen of the Law are determined to put in force their Judiciary Bill which puts the court more in the power of the Judges. Thus in the General Government & in the States every attempt to maintain a Legislature independent of the Judiciary is frustrated.''

Also, Ind. Chronicle, September 22, 1808. ''The great object contemplated by the Federalists is to make the judiciary the permanent branch of government—that all laws should be subject to the control of the judges—that the Legislature should be subordinate to the control of the Judiciary. . . . What section of the constitution gives the judges a right to decide on the constitutionality of the laws? . . . The right assumed by the judges to set aside the laws is nowhere recognized in the constitution,'' etc.

[80] Col. Centinel, July 12, 1806, quotes a Republican Fourth of July toast at Lynn and comments on its dangerous principles. ''The Judiciary— Periodical election of Judges, the best pledge of their good behavior; may this mode of appointment become constitutional in state and nation.''

The election of all officers, to fill all parts of the government, is the natural genius that presides over the United States, and if my conviction is just, there will be spasms and commotions in the states until such an amendment takes place. . . . If men are incompetent to elect their judges, they are equally incompetent to appoint others to do it for them. . . . But, tho' the people have this Judiciary check against the usurpations of the Legislature, what check have they against the usurpation of the Judiciary? When Judges set up their opinion on the constitution in opposition to the legislature, and in opposition to the great mass of the people, who can check them? The people cannot, for they have no direct voice in setting them up or taking them down. The Legislature cannot, except by impeachment, which in such cases would be no more than a whistle. The executive cannot for they hold their office by a tenure which the executive cannot destroy. . . . My age authorizes me to say that the leading doctrine of the American Revolution has been that responsibility was the best expedient to keep men honest. And why this maxim should be inverted in the Judiciary establishment alone I never could see. . . . The judges would not only feel the importance of judicial officers, but also the salutary obligation to be men. A judicial monarch is a character as abhorrent as an executive or legislative monarch in my view.[81]

The frequent prosecution of Republicans for libel and other political offenses was a source of irritation.[82] The famous Austin tragedy in Boston, which grew out

[81] An Elective Judiciary, with other things recommended in a Speech, pronounced at Cheshire, July 4, 1805. By John Leland, Pittsfield, 1805. Am. Ant. Soc. Library. Leland in the course of his speech also attacks ''the host of lawyers who infest our land like the swarms of locusts in Egypt, and eat up every green thing.''

[82] GREENE, Religious Liberty in Conn., 403, 437. Am. Mercury, January 30, 1806. ''Both parties in the State have an idea that our Courts lean in their decisions towards federalism, and that a republican cannot be tried by his peers.''

Cf. BENTLEY, Diary, III, 30. ''The Republicans should not try Courts of Justice so called unnecessarily.''

of the political struggle in that city, gave further aggravation to the Republican belief that they were regarded as an inferior class by their opponents and not entitled to the ordinary rights of citizens.[83] "By federal management, treason, murder, sedition and libel have dwindled, either into simple misdemeanors, or justifiable exercises of the liberty of action and freedom of speech; provided the perpetrators are federal and the objects of their attempts republican."[84]

With such feeling as the animus of the Republican movement, it was inevitable that any restrictions on the right of suffrage should arouse opposition. If there was a demand for wider popular control of the government, by a party generally opposed to propertied interests, it was intolerable that large numbers of citizens should be deprived of voting because of property qualifications. The party doctrines on this matter further illustrate their essential differences.

Vermont had no property qualification. New Hampshire allowed every person to vote who paid a tax, however small, or did militia duty.[85] The rapid growth of the Republican party in these states may have been influenced by this fact. In the three southern New England states, property qualifications existed. In Connecticut the opposition to the system was strenuous, and the radical character of Republicanism in this state was early exhibited in a movement for the aboli-

[83] AMORY, Sullivan, II, 163-189, gives a full account of this affair. Selfridge, a prominent Federalist lawyer, shot and killed Chas. Austin, son of Benj. Austin, a Republican pamphleteer and political writer. He was acquitted after a trial before Justice Parsons, in which the leading Federalist legal talent appeared in his defense.

[84] Ind. Chronicle, February 22, 1808.

[85] Cf. BENTLEY, Diary, III, 415. "New Hampshire makes every soldier a voter, & residents two years in U. S. A. This is the true spirit of elections."

tion of this requirement. A special incentive was furnished by the belief that under the Election Law of 1801 the Federalists were regularly refusing admission to those justly entitled to vote.[86] The demand for universal suffrage accompanied that for a new constitution and carried dismay to the upholders of the old order.[87] At the fall session of the legislature a bill was introduced by a Republican member, extending the right to vote to all citizens of the state whom the selectmen and civil authority of the town should certify to be "of good moral character and peaceable behavior."[88]

The debate on this measure is an admirable illustration of a fundamental difference in the parties. The author of the bill explained its purpose and argued that persons paying taxes should have a voice in the government as a mere matter of justice. The speeches of Noah Webster and Ephraim Kirby, the latter a prominent Republican and candidate for governor, are of chief interest. The admission of too many people to the right of suffrage, who had no settled habitation, and nothing which could induce them to wish for the peace of the state, had been the ruin of all popular government. "We had better adhere to the regulations of our ancestors." To Kirby's rejoinder that the admission of freemen would still depend on the consent of

[86] Am. Mercury, October 25, November 1, 8, 1804, May 16, 1805.

[87] Conn. Courant, April 6, 1803. "We also know that our clergy and our religion are denounced by our own Democrats in terms of blasphemy. A State Constitution is boldly called for, universal suffrage is claimed as a natural right. Paine and his writings are extolled above the Saviour and his gospel." "Federal Freeman." See also February 16, 23, March 2.

[88] This bill and the accompanying debate were published in Am. Mercury, December 2, 1802. The subject had already been discussed in the press. Cf. the following, *ibid.*, September 16. "Virginia disfranchises the poor black man. Connecticut disfranchises the poor white man. Virginia does not rail at Connecticut for saying her blacks are treated like cattle. Connecticut rails at Virginia for saying her poor are treated like blacks."

town authorities, and that besides, every member had more valuable rights for which he claimed protection than those of property, he replied that the bill in question prostrated the wealth of individuals "to the rapaciousness of a merciless gang who have nothing to lose. It opens the door for electioneering, for men of no property are liable to influence." The avenues must not be opened, for the number of persons without property was certain to increase, while the observation that the poor have lives, limbs, and reputation to be protected does not apply. "Our laws principally respect property; that is their great object; and it is very improper that it should be at the direction and disposal of those who have no interest in it." The bill was defeated but the subject was constantly discussed in succeeding years.

In 1806 the Republican side of the argument was again laid before the state in a series of papers on "Universal Suffrage," some extracts of which are worth quoting.

Could the poor of this pious state rise up in judgment against the rich and have some other Court than a Court of the rich to try the cause they would soon be admitted to some portion of political being. The poor could plead that they have fought and bled for their country, that some of them have been plundered by the rich of seven years' hard earnings, that they are now paying taxes and doing duty in the militia; but the reply of the rich would be, "We have suffered you to live and have protected you from your worst enemies, yourselves."[89]

Property, sacred property, is regarded as all in all, by our federal politicians, and a want of it implies according to their catechism, a want of sense, of industry, of morals, and religion; yet the Savior of the world and his disciples probably did not possess as much of this world's goods as would entitle one man to be made free in Connecticut. It is astonishing that

[89] Am. Mercury, January 2, 1806.

among people professing as much religion as the Federalists do, property should be placed over everything else.[90]

And again:

The great alarm about this is, lest the poor should gain the advantage of the rich; but all the laws in the world were never able to give the poor one tenth of their rights.[91]

In Massachusetts the subject does not appear to have attracted much attention before 1809.[92] In this year the Gore administration passed a law raising the requirements of the law of March 23, 1786, adding to the required payment of poll tax and an amount equal to two thirds thereof, a sum equal to a poll tax.[93] The new requirement was regarded as a blow to the Republicans as the protests show.

Nothing but the full exercise and fruition of suffrage can make a man rationally and politically free. . . . The language of a majority of our general court is,—Thou poor! thy hallowed right of suffrage is taken from thee and given to others; this hook we are pleased to put into thy nose, and this bridle into thy jaws. . . . Notwithstanding the hard times and the difficulty of collecting taxes—notwithstanding other states are lowering the suffrage—notwithstanding popular approval of the old law—still our elective franchise must be contracted and

[90] *Ibid.*, January 9.

[91] *Ibid.*, January 16, See also January 23. For a similar attack on the Federalist theory that power should follow property, see N. H. Gazette, September 18, 1804.

[92] In 1804, when the Massachusetts legislature was discussing the proposed amendment to the U. S. constitution to abolish slave representation, the Ind. Chronicle, August 23, 1804, states that there were 27,000 men in Massachusetts not entitled to vote because of the property qualifications, and ''according to the new freak of Federalism ought to be excluded from the census on which representation is founded. . . . the constitution ought to be amended so as to exclude them.''

[93] General Laws, 209, 1809, chap. 26 (repealed chap. 40).

mutilated; a new law must be worked into being to wrest from poorer people one of their most essential immunities.[94]

The election of the Gerry administration changed the situation and one of the most noteworthy acts of that active administration was the passage, June 18, 1811, of a universal suffrage law.[95] "They have extended the right of suffrage in the choice of town officers to all persons (except paupers) of twenty-one years of age and upwards, who shall have resided a year in any town, and in all other town affairs to any person paying a poll tax; thereby taking away the pecuniary qualifications which have been required since the year 1692, and giving to every transient person, without property, character, or any fixed place of abode, the right of voting away the property of his neighbor in town affairs in which he has no permanent interest or concern."[96] This is the language of a Federalist convention; the Republicans defended the measure as a mere act of common justice to a large class of citizens "many of whom had assisted in the establishment of independence."[97] In Rhode Island there was a movement under way in 1811 to repeal the property qualification. "The right to vote is a natural property, any person who would require property of another kind is guilty of oppression." "Every person doing road work, paying taxes or doing militia duty should vote."[98] In March a

[94] E. Argus, January 18, 1810. "Republican."

[95] General Laws, 278, 1811, chap. 9.

[96] Col. Centinel, March 21, 1812. Resolutions of Southern Senatorial District.

Cf. *ibid.*, July 31, 1812. "As equally subversive of our civil institutions we deprecate the principles of universal suffrage uncontrolled by such restraints as are imposed by the spirit of the constitution."

[97] Ind. Chronicle, March 19, 1812. Resolutions of Norfolk County Convention.

[98] R. I. Republican, February 21, 1811. "Republican Farmer's Resolutions." See also March 6, for article by "Freeman."

bill granting this demand passed the Senate with only two dissenting votes but the House postponed it for further consideration,[99] and the outbreak of war and the depression of Republican strength for the next few years caused the subject to be dropped.

The Federalist opposition to the demands for a more democratic administration was not unnatural. The state governments had apparently been conducted with honesty and efficiency. To be sure, they showed an irritating confidence that no other party could conduct a government with the same qualities.[100] Two incidents in Massachusetts seemed to lend color to this belief. The first Republican state treasurer, ex-Congressman Skinner, was alleged to have looted the treasury of $60,000 during his brief term of office.[101] Two years later another prominent Republican, Barnabas Bidwell, was forced to leave the state because of defalcations while treasurer of Berkshire. "Such are your idols, O Democracy!" exclaimed the *Centinel*. The deep aversion with which the Federalists regarded Pennsylvania where the Republicans had early secured control would seem to indicate that New England was on a decidedly higher plane politically,[102] and perhaps helps

[99] *Ibid.*, March 13.

[100] Naïve expressions of Federalist opinion occur in the following. Col. Centinel, November 13, 1805. "It is believed that Federalism is increasing in Rhode Island, for encouragement is given to Public Schools, new houses of public worship are building; new roads are opening, and the industry and commerce of the state is reviving."

Ibid., May 3, 1806. "The Rhode Island democrats are more careful for the preservation of their money than their liberties." They had elected a Federalist state treasurer. The Vermont "democrats" were said to have taken similar precautions in 1804. See Pol. Observatory, November 3.

[101] MORSE, Fed. Party in Mass., 182.

[102] Portsmouth Oracle, February 27, 1802. "Mifflin prepared the way for McKean and both were harbingers of the great Jefferson. . . . Mr. Jefferson is busily engaged in restoring harmony to social intercourse. After we have had the benefit of his labors another year we shall be pre-

to account for the dread with which they viewed "the impending rule of democracy—more tyrannous and more cruel than Egyptian bondage."[103]

The statistics which have been given elsewhere form a sufficient proof of the success of the Republican propaganda. What Bentley wrote of Salem in 1806 would doubtless be true of many other towns had they had such an industrious chronicler to record the fact. "While Salem was under the greatest Aristocracy in New England few men thought & the few directed the many. Now the Aristocracy is gone & the many govern. It is plain it must require considerable time to give common knowledge to the people."[104]

pared for the political millenium which now reigns in the city of New York and the state of Pennsylvania." Cf. GIBBS, Memoirs, II, 399. "McKean's administration has brought every scoundrel who can read or write into office, or expectation of one, and the residue of Democrats, with the joy and ferocity of the damned, are enjoying the mortification of the few honest men and Federalists, and exalting their own hopes of preferment, and that of their friends, in proportion as they dismiss the fear of the gallows." Tracy to Wolcott, August 7, 1799. Also, Conn. Courant, April 8, 1807, points to New York and Pennsylvania for "examples of Democratic government."

[103] Col. Centinel, August 11, 1804.

[104] Diary, III, 265, December 2, 1806. Cf. Ind. Chronicle, February 2, 1804. In reference to New Hampshire a writer states: "The resolution which called the Democratic power into action has repressed aristocratic spirit. The honors and emoluments of office are more generally diffused, the people enjoy more equal privileges and after long dissensions are better united."

CHAPTER VII

REPUBLICANISM AND RELIGIOUS LIBERTY

In 1805 Alexander Wolcott, the so-called state manager of the Connecticut Republicans, in a circular letter to his local henchmen warned them that the privileged orders were numerous and powerful, and described "the standing army of federalism" as composed of the clergy, lawyers, physicians, judges, justices and military officers.[1] The clergy, it is to be noticed, are given first place in this arrangement. Perhaps—to continue Wolcott's figure—they might be considered as the heavy artillery of the standing army. They underwent the same attack which the Republicans directed against the lawyers, judges, and propertied classes, and from the importance of their position in New England society this phase of the Republican movement is of special interest.

The Congregational Church was one of the fundamental institutions of New England. The social and political life of the towns centered around the church, and the ministers had been, from the earliest settlement of the country, the leaders in public affairs. "In the settlement of no other country," remarks one writer, "perhaps that of Canaan excepted, was religion so much the object as in New England."[2] The uniformity of religious belief until almost the end of the eighteenth

[1] This circular appears in Am. Mercury, March, 20, 1806, and contains an interesting summary of political conditions and Republican plans of campaign.

[2] Ind. Chronicle, July 4, 1799.

century was one of the causes of New England's peculiar solidarity. The political affiliations of the clergy were bound to be a subject of vital importance as soon as a well-defined party system should develop.

There was not much doubt as to which party the clergy would support. They had been energetic supporters of the Revolution, although the Republicans afterwards made the charge that their attitude was due rather to the fear of an Episcopal Establishment under royal protection, than to any love for the principles of the great struggle.[3] In the dark years which followed the close of the war they had proved firm friends of law and order and had thrown their influence on the side of the government during the Shays Rebellion.[4] They were as a rule strongly in favor of the adoption of the Federal Constitution. With the rise of party in 1792 the clergy, almost from the first, tended to act with the Federalists. The sympathy of the Republicans for Revolutionary France was a factor in determining the attitude of the clergy. French influence was blamed for the undoubted increase of irreligion which had been alarming the churches since the end of the Revolution.[5]

---

[3] *Ibid.*, September 2, 1805. Quoted from Pol. Observatory. ''The Congregational churches in this country had been democracies and they were urgently opposed to the attempts before made to establish episcopalian churches, because they proceeded from the king. . . . Yet democracy did not sit easy on all the Congregational clergy after the Revolution: the danger of Episcopalian churches being established with precedency, was then taken away and the Congregationalists had a clear precedence in the state.'' Cf. ''The Deceptive Arts of Demagogues,'' Am. Mercury, December 27, 1804. ''The writer says that 700 Clergymen were Whigs in the last war. We say that 500 are now Tories. . . . They and their boys could not be supreme, if King George was supreme and the Episcopal Clergy received stipends from England.''

[4] MORSE, Fed. Party in Mass., 95. See also ''A Defense of the Clergy of New England,'' Col. Centinel, January 5, 1805.

[5] GREENE, Religious Liberty in Conn., 408-410. MORSE, Fed. Party in Mass., 88-115.

By 1795 their position was well established as the leading Federalist influence, and for the next twenty years there was an intimate relation between religion and politics throughout New England.

The value of clerical support to the Federalists was generally recognized among their opponents. "An old Tory openly asserted in this town [Boston] that the aristocratic party could never gain an interest in America until they enlisted the clergy on their side," says a writer in 1795.[6] Again, a few years later, another remarks in the Pittsfield *Sun,* the Republican organ of western Massachusetts: "May kingly government never get footing here. I am sure it never will without the aid of Clergymen. May civil and religious intolerance never flourish here, I know they will not without the culture of the Clergy.'"[7] Still another, "It is a conspicuous fact that they have done more to stop progress of republican light than any other class of men.'"[8] Jefferson, undoubtedly the shrewdest political observer of the day, recognized their influence, and to its absence in Rhode Island he attributed the early "regeneration" of that state.[9] Writing to Pierpont Edwards of conditions in Connecticut he remarked: "Their steady habits exclude the advances of information and they seem exactly where they were when they separated from the saints of Oliver Cromwell. And there your clergy will always keep them if they can.'"[10]

[6] Ind. Chronicle, October 5, 1795. See also July 20.

Ibid., January 14, 1805. "There was always in New England a respectable opposition to federal principles, and nothing less than a combination of monied men and priests prevented the downfall of those principles in that quarter long since."

[7] Quoted by Am. Mercury, January 14, 1805.

[8] *Ibid.,* December 27, 1804.

[9] FORD, Jefferson Writings, VIII, 48.

[10] *Ibid.,* 75. Jefferson to Edwards, July 21, 1801.

Cf. *ibid.,* 41. Jefferson to Gerry, March 29, 1801. "Your part of the

The political sermon, especially that delivered on Fast and Thanksgiving Days, was a powerful weapon in the hands of the clergy. A vast number of these addresses has come down to us; they are characterized by almost uniform pessimism and narrowness of view. Jefferson was the object of a great deal of abuse.[11] His well-known liberality in religious views and his fondness for French literature and philosophy made him an object of suspicion. He also made no attempt to conceal his dislike for the privileged position of the New England church, and always considered his work in breaking down the Episcopal Establishment in his own state as one of his greatest services to mankind.[12]

The union of politics and religion always appeared at the annual inauguration ceremonies. Here were preached the election sermons which the irreverent Abraham Bishop described as having "a little of governor, a little of council, a little of congress, much of puffing, much of politics and a very little religion—a

Union tho' as absolutely republican as ours, had drunk deeper of the delusion, and is therefore slower in recovering from it. The ægis of government, and the temples of religion and justice, have all been prostituted there, to toll us back to the times when we burnt witches."

[11] ADAMS, U. S., I, 80-82. Cf. BENTLEY, Diary, III, 208. "The political conduct of the clergy is no where so insolent as in Connecticut. In that state a Southington pastor at Branford, scrupled not to call the President, a debauchee, an infidel, and a Liar. But these excesses are less worthy of notice when the reputation of the inferior Clergy is known." Such sermons were sometimes used as campaign documents. Ibid., II, 423, April 3, 1802. "The last day of asking, & political interests were never so seriously engaged among us. Emmons' Fast Sermon describing Jefferson under the odious name of Jeroboam, was distributed gratis. The Republicans had no aid in this way, except what an extract from Dr. Maclintock's letter in the Register could afford them." Copies of this "Jeroboam" sermon are in Am. Ant. Soc. Library.

[12] Writing to Levi Lincoln, January 1, 1802, and enclosing an address to the Baptists, Jefferson states: "I know it will give great offense to the New England Clergy; but the advocate of religious freedom is to expect neither peace nor forgiveness from them."

strange compost, like a carrot pye, having so little of
the ingredients of the vegetable, that the cook must
christen it.''[13]   A Republican summary of the election
sermon of 1804 at Hartford is interesting. ''We godly
ministers who are hand and glove with the men in
power, are vastly holy men; we understand all God's
purposes in respect to the political as well as the moral
concerns of this world, and we know Mr. Jefferson is
in office contrary to the divine will, or as a punishment
for the sins of this people, and we know that God took
great delight in Mr. Adams and his navy and army
and taxes, and that he suffered him to go out of office
to punish us for our rebellion, and we know that he will
finally raise up Pinckney, or King, or Hamilton, or some
other friend of Zion, and the Clergy, to be at the head
of us, and we shall yet be a great and holy nation.''[14]
To one who has read some of these addresses this will
not seem an unfair description.

The vast majority of the Congregational clergy were
Federalists, although two, Allen of Pittsfield and Bentley of Salem, were prominent Republicans. There were
some minor exceptions. Bradford of Rowley had
preached a violent tirade against Washington's administration in 1795 and had in consequence been ostra-
cized by his clerical brethren.[15] Stanley Griswold in
Connecticut was practically forced from the ministry

13 Wallingford Oration, 45.

14 Am. Mercury, June 14, 1804.

15 MORSE, Fed. Party in Mass., 134. Cf. BENTLEY, Diary, II, 129,
February 25, 1795. ''Subscriptions about for the sermon preached on the
last Thanksgiving by Dr. Bernard of this Town. . . . It is said that Bradford of Rowley has given one of pure democracy, that several will be
printed in Boston & that a counterpart is wanted. . . . The Clergy are
now the tools of the Federalists and Thanksgiving Sermons are in the order
of the Day.'' Ibid., 156. ''Bradford of Rowley, has suffered much from
his antifederal sermon. The Association have disapproved of it, & have
received some acknowledgment.''

and became editor of a Republican newspaper, the *Political Observatory*, at Walpole, N. H.[16]

Bentley quotes as evidence of "the persecuting spirit which has troubled the political world," one of the Federalist toasts at a Fourth of July celebration at Salem. "The Clergy, a chearing Luminary whose grateful influence is not to be impaired by the few spots which partially obscure it."[17] He himself was one of the "spots."

The attitude of the clergy could not but arouse the bitterest opposition among Republicans. The party stood for a wider freedom; the domineering tone of the clergy forced them to take the offensive, and from 1794 on, the Republicans were the champions of religious freedom and the enemies of clerical privilege.[18] Dr. Morse, one of the leading Federalist preachers of Massachusetts, had described the clergy of Connecticut as those who "numerous, able, harmonious, and very respectable as a body, have hitherto preserved a kind of aristocratical balance in the very democratical government of the state. This has happily operated as a check upon the overbearing spirit of democracy."[19] This description was generally applied by the Republicans to the order throughout New England. "Aristocracy" was a word which would stir the wrath of every Republican; to have the clergy openly so called by one of their own number was a challenge which was readily accepted.[20] The effect on the position of the clergy was

[16] Portsmouth Oracle, July 21, 1804, has an attack on this paper and its editor.

[17] Diary, III, 170. The Portsmouth Oracle, March 19, 1814, speaks of Bentley as "the Archbishop of Democracy in New England."

[18] Cf. MORSE, Fed. Party in Mass., 129.

[19] Universal Geography, 4th ed., 435.

[20] Bentley records a characteristic incident, which shows the aggressiveness of the New England parson, who was never noted for meekness and

bound to be serious and Bentley writes in 1795 expressing his fear that the rash zeal with which the clergy had
gone into the political controversy would have evil
results. The French clergy had suffered severely from
their failure to "continue with the people."[21] As he
anticipated, the New England clergy soon began to pay
the penalty for a similar failure.

The Republicans, especially in Boston, had begun to
attack the political activities of the clergy at the time
of the Jay Treaty excitement, and for several years
scarcely a number of the *Independent Chronicle* is free
from letters or other articles assailing them.[22] Republicanism in this way probably came to be associated in
many minds with enmity to religion. The members of
the party deeply resented the conduct of the ministers.
Dr. Ames writes on one occasion: "Proclamation for
political fast through U. S. many People provoked
thereat. The People of Dorchester it is said intend to
work on high ways that day 25 inst. others say they'll
take no notice of it, but curiosity to hear the political

long-suffering. Diary, II, 272. June 24, 1798. ''I tarried & spent the
Sunday at Marlborough. . . . In this town french influence has prevailed,
tho' now abating. On the national fast, an English Flag was displayed on
the Parson's Barn. His discretion has not been seen in political discus-
sions. . . .''

[21] Diary, II, 130. Cf. 266. ''Arts are used to engage the Clergy in
the English interest. The french friends were said to dispose their talents
as usually below mediocrity. But the Clergy will not be supported in
Republics by public favour only for State purposes & if a few insinuations
are to decide them, they will have them plentifully from the party they
abandon.''

[22] For examples of such attacks see July 20, 23, 1795, June 24, December 6, 31, 1798, April 18, October 28, 1799. See September 22, 1800, a
letter from ''Philanthropos'' objecting to this policy. ''Very few numbers
of the Chronicle have been free from abuse of the clergy and their followers, since Osgood preached his sermon so obnoxious to exclusive patriots
and Republicans.'' This famous sermon was preached November 20, 1794.
See MORSE, Fed. Party in Mass., 126.

Drum draws people against their intention. . . . At Charlestown half the people left the meeting, one telling the minister, Morse, there was no truth in what he said.''[23] With such a feeling prevalent, many of the leading Republicans became open enemies of the church, and their newspapers conducted a campaign against it. In Connecticut, Bishop, perhaps the cleverest of the Republican orators and pamphleteers, took delight in baiting "the old firm of Moses and Aaron.''[24] Levi Lincoln also became a dangerous foe, his position as a member of the Cabinet, drawing special attention to his words.[25]

The stand which the Republicans took in opposition to clerical influence insured them the support of a growing body in New England, the minor dissenting sects. There was a marked increase in these bodies, especially the Baptist, during and after the Revolutionary War.[26] The religious condition of New England after the war was far from satisfactory, and the desire to combat

[23] Diary, April 10, 1799.

[24] An oration in honor of the election of President Jefferson and the peaceable acquisition of Louisiana, delivered at the national festival in Hartford, on the eleventh of May, 1804, 20. See also 17, 18, 23.

[25] Letters to the People, By a Farmer. Salem, 1802.

Cf. BENTLEY, Diary, II, 407. ''A most serious Dispute has been opened in the Gazette in regard to the Clergy. The clergy had so plainly spoken & written upon the subject of the present administration, that a writer said to be the Attorney General of the U. S. under the signature of a 'Farmer,' in his 10 numbers has openly attacked them. The blow is serious, & the more the Clergy & their friends attempt to defend themselves, the more severe are the strokes upon them. This subject never was so freely handled in New England & never did the Clergy suffer a more serious diminution of their influence & of their power.''

For interesting attacks on the clergy, see also Am. Mercury, January 21, 1803, for quotation from Pittsfield Sun. Also N. H. Gazette, February 22, 1803.

[26] BURRAGE, History of the Baptists in New England, 101. ''The struggle fostered the spirit of civil and religious liberty and so opened the way for the reception of Baptist principles.''

the influence of French philosophy led all denominations to engage in aggressive religious work.[27]   In 1789
Jesse Lee began to preach Methodism in Connecticut
and within the next few years the denomination appeared in all parts of New England.[28]   The formation
of new religious parties was almost as disturbing to
existing New England life as that of political parties.
In 1794 a writer makes a long complaint against the
conduct of the Methodists and "their impudence in
breaking into other men's enclosures," their extravagance and noise, and "their practice of travelling in
droves and companies on the Sabbath day, trampling
upon all law and order and disturbing serious people
under pretense of liberty of conscience."[29]   The Baptist
and Methodist preachers who labored in New England
in these years were subject to constant annoyance,
amounting at times to persecution.[30]

The latter years of the eighteenth and the first years
of the nineteenth century were marked by extensive
revivals, in which the Baptists and Methodists made
great gains.[31]   Such events were common in the newer
settlements and here the strength of these denominations was marked.[32]   Timothy Dwight noted, while
traveling in New Hampshire, that religious difficulties
and divisions were very common in new settlements

[27] GREENE, Religious Liberty in Conn., 414-415.

[28] STEVENS, Memorials of the Introduction of Methodism into the Eastern States, 45 ff.

[29] Am. Mercury, September 22.

[30] BURRAGE, History of Baptists, 119. STEVENS, Memorials, 68, 95, 135.

[31] GREENE, Religious Liberty in Conn., 415.

[32] For accounts of revivals at Wethersfield, Vt., Spooner's Vt. Journal,
November 27, 1804. Norton, Mass., July 23. In Maine E. Argus, August
9, September 30, 1804. These give interesting descriptions of the scenes
at camp meetings, resembling those enacted in Kentucky a short time
before. See also Col. Centinel, August 1, 1804, for accounts from Vermont.
An account of the great revivals of 1798-1799 appears in the following

where "the planters coming together more by casualty than by design, bring with them all their former habits of thinking. Their religious principles, their views of ecclesiastical discipline, and their scheme of morals, must, of course, be various."[33] Vermont and the District of Maine were filled with such people. Thomas Robbins on a missionary tour of the Onion River settlements in Vermont, writes in 1799: "People in this State do not appear to be so much infected with infidelity, as erroneous views in religion. The Methodists have a pretty strong hold at [list of towns], but not much at the northward of these places. The disorganizing principles of the Baptists do considerable damage."[34] Another Congregational missionary in Maine, after uncomplimentary reference to the Baptists, writes in 1800, "Want of learning, religion, and love of order suffers the people of Maine to be imposed on by quacks in divinity, politics and physic."[35]

Bentley gives an interesting record of events in the religious world during these years. His viewpoint is that of a liberal Congregationalist and a Republican. In 1803 he writes: "The Baptists are a growing sect, because their rite is so definite as to make a more easy distinction in the public mind, than any doctrines can, and this distinction gains a ready exemption from parish taxes. The Baptists grow not rapidly in great Towns, where such exceptions are unnecessary."[36] A year later:

pamphlet: A brief Account of the late Revivals in Religion, in a number of towns in the New England States, and also in Nova Scotia. Windsor, Vt., 1800. Am. Ant. Soc. Library. Most of this work describes events in Maine and Vermont.

33 Travels, II, 88.
34 Diary of Thomas Robbins, D. D., I, 90.
35 Memoir and Journals of Rev. Paul Coffin, D. D., Collections of the Maine Historical Society, IV, 404.
36 Diary, III, 4.

"On the subject of Consociation of Churches nothing was ripened into a plan. . . . The truth seems to be
the influx of Methodists & Baptists has disturbed all
the Clergy. These sects have an evident co-operation
not assisted by the laws but by their condition in the
minority."[37]   In 1805: "Sects are in all their glory in
New England & through the United States. They are
as thick as the gulls upon our sandbar as hungry & as
useless."[38]   And so the record continues. In 1808 he
writes: "The various sects have prevailed so far in
Massachusetts as to embrace a great part of the population. For tho' societies are not formed & houses of
worship built yet in all our incorporations a number
may be found who are prevented only from want of some
enterprising man to engage in the work of seperation."[39]

Stevens states that, during the first ten years of the
century, the Methodist denomination doubled its districts, circuits, and ministry, and more than trebled its
membership, the latter rising from 5839 to 17,592, an
average increase of nearly 100 per month.[40] The Baptists gains were also very considerable. Of approximately five hundred churches which were in existence
in 1813, 124 had been organized since 1800.[41]

The increase of these denominations had an important effect on political events. The Congregational
Church as an institution stood for Federalism. Now
there was a great body in the community hostile to it on
religious grounds; it was natural that they should enlist
with its political enemies.

[37] *Ibid.*, 91.
[38] *Ibid.*, 207.
[39] *Ibid.*, 345.
See also 36, 75, 76, 82, 91, 101, 157, 179, 192, 207, 212, 503, 506, 512.
[40] Memorials, 2d Series, 489, 490. This volume gives in great detail the
history of Methodist activity in this period.
[41] BENEDICT, History of the Baptists, II, 497-508.

There was no friendly feeling between the regular and dissenting bodies and this probably increased political animosity. "It has been my lot for thirteen years past to be opposed by the clergy, from whom I have received the most abusive treatment I ever met with. . . . According to the best information I have, there is not so useless and hurtful a set of public men in our country as the clergy. A man needs not a great share of knowledge to see that as a body of men they are professed enemies of our Republican government, and open enemies of the President."[42] These are the words of one Baptist leader. Says another in an oration in honor of Jefferson's second election, "In the first place, does not an unhallowed unconverted lover of filthy lucre, go to college and learn the art of keeping the people in ignorance, and then come forth A.M. after receiving the mark in the forehead and in the right hand, tantamount to Popish priest?"[43] The regular clergy were not less severe in describing their opponents. A missionary in Maine naïvely remarks of the Methodists: "They make very many and injurious divisions among Christians. . . . I think our new settlements are much to be pitied, as they are overrun with Methodist teachers,"[44] and earlier, speaking of the town of Mount Vernon, "This is a place of horse jockeying, taverning, law suits, etc., not affording hearers

[42] The Clergyman's Looking Glass or Ancient and Modern Things Contrasted. By Elias Smith, Boston, 1804. See also, by same author, A Discourse delivered at Jefferson Hall, Thanksgiving Day, November 25, 1802. Portsmouth, N. H., 1802. A Discourse on Government and Religion, delivered at Gray, Maine, July 14, 1810. Portland, 1810. Am. Ant. Soc. Library.

[43] A Discourse, delivered at Lebanon, Conn., on the fourth of March, 1805, before a large Concourse of respectable citizens met in honor of the late presidential Election of Thomas Jefferson. By Elias Nehemiah Dodge of Middletown. Norwich, 1805, 27.

[44] P. COFFIN, Journal. Coll. Me. Hist. Soc., IV, 334.

even for Baptists and Methodists.''[45]   Another minister writes: ''You may see them increasing their numbers by readily admitting such as are troublesome persons in society, such as have been cast out of regular churches, and such as have taken affront at some just reproof from their paster. . . . They first endeavor to make proselytes of the weak and ignorant.''[46]

These last words are rather significant.   There is considerable evidence that the sectaries appealed to a somewhat lower social class.   Timothy Dwight noted that there was a great dearth of educated men among the Baptists.[47]   Kendall, whose opinion as a foreigner is of special value, noted that their followers were of the most ignorant and illiterate part of the population.[48] Bentley furnishes suggestive comments.   Speaking of the difficulties of a brother minister, ''the ignorant sects, & the Baptists at present are of this class, draw away the ignorant of a very small parish from him.''[49] The sectaries had been carrying on a religious agitation, ''but it evidently subsides.   It seems to have spread as far as education will suffer it and the tide must take another turn.''   Again—the town of Beverly—''the majority of the population are in the humblest grades

45 *Ibid.*, 306.

46 The Christian Doctrines stated, and False Teachers Discovered, in the Sermons by William Riddell, A. B., Pastor of the Congregational Church in Bristol, Me.   Wiscasset, 1800, 19-22.   Am. Ant. Soc. Library.

Cf. the following in Dartmouth Gazette, November 18, 1807, relative to the recent passage of a religious liberty law in Vermont.   ''The situation of the clergy must be very discouraging. . . . The way will be more freely opened for the inroads of those ignorant imposters, those disorganizing vagabonds, those straggling pests of good order, who go about under the name of preachers, leading astray the weak and incautious and whose base hypocrisy or wild fanaticism have already had considerable influence throughout the community.''

47 Travels, I, 177; IV, 161.

43 Travels, III, 107.

49 Diary, III, 106.

of information. The Baptist minister expects a harvest.''[50] The tendency of this class of people to enter the Republican ranks is quite in accord with the general fact already noted, that parties were based to a considerable degree on social lines.

That the minor sects were almost wholly Republican is a matter on which evidence is abundant.[51] "That party [the Republican] has been continually denouncing the clergy of regular standing as the friends of monarchy and charging them with intermeddling with politics with which they have no concern. But what is their conduct with the Baptists? it is unnecessary to answer—everyone in New Hampshire where there are any of that sect, knows their conduct.''[52] A few years earlier a Federalist address to the Baptists had gone the rounds of the press urging them to repent of their political errors.[53] The comment on this by Republicans is suggestive. "The writer intimates, that though the Baptists are friends to religion, yet at the same time they are friendly to a political sentiment called Democracy. . . . Remember my Brethren, that the truth you believe, is not supported by the friends of State Religion. . . .''[54] Again, a year later the same paper says, "Let the Baptists, Methodists, Quakers, and all other distinctions look to the designs of the Federalists and adhere to Jefferson.''[55]

Bentley's evidence is especially full and valuable. He is always inclined to regard the growth of the dissenting

[50] *Ibid.*, III, 515. See also 134.
[51] See GREENE, Religious Liberty in Conn., 407. PLUMER, Plumer, 186.
[52] Portsmouth Oracle, March 11, 1809.
[53] Conn. Courant, March 28, 1804.
[54] N. H. Gazette, August 21, 1804.
[55] *Ibid.*, August 13, 1805.
See also Portland Gazette, October 22, 1804, March 25, 1805. R. I. Republican, January 2, 23, 1811.

element as due to political reasons. ''The Baptists by attaching themselves to the present administration have gained great success in the U. S. & greater in New England than any sect since the settlement, even beyond comparison. This seems to be a warning to the Churches of the other denominations. . . . The president is in full consent with them upon the use of civil power in the State. The Baptists are in their constituencies more republican than the Methodists, though hardly much more join their profession.''[56] . . . Later on, ''The Congregationalists begin to be alarmed at the great progress of the Anabaptists, but the progress is not from their opinions, but from their political situation to oppose the busy Clergymen who are tools of the Anti-Jefferson party.''[57] A suggestive comment, ''The Methodist minister, Mr. James profits by the Republican temper of Lynn, as did the stupid Pottle, a Baptist, at Ipswich.''[58]

The Baptists have always been friends of liberty and

[56] Diary, II, 409. Cf. III, 65. ''Never has there been greater religious convulsions in the public mind since the Revolution. The methodists by their manner of supplying preachers have had great advantages in our new settlements. The active part the regular clergy have taken with the opposition of the present administration, has thrown all the discontented into the sect of the Baptists. . . . The introduction of laymen as they are called, or zealous persons without a public or regular education has much contributed to inflame zeal, & everywhere we find convulsions, separations, zeal and spiritual gifts celebrated.'' See also 82.

[57] Ibid., 419.

[58] Ibid., III, 170. Dr. Ames in his Diary tells of a violent quarrel in Parish meeting over the choice of a minister and how ''F. Ames and the lawyers'' dictated to the rest. His illustrious brother ''harrangued them pathetically about pious forefathers'' and ''crammed the Priest down their throats tail foremost.'' December 20, 1802. The following entry occurs a few weeks later, February 10, 1803. ''I and others having joined the Episcopal Church, they exult at our departure, as I hear, as not more to be troubled with our opposition. . . . Every infamous slander against Seceders is raised to justify themselves in their oppression & tyranny, that drove us to withdraw.''

the following description of their constitution, from a
contemporary pamphlet, explains why there was a
natural attraction between the sect and the Republican
movement. The writer describes the Baptist constitution
as follows:

> The source of religious liberty—the real friend of civil
> liberty—approves the first principles of the American revolu-
> tion, constitution and government—and all measures of admin-
> istration which are founded upon them; and earnestly prays
> for the bestowment of these blessings on all mankind—makes
> allowance, however, for common mistakes—is highly suspicious
> of federalism—having stood in front of the battle against ene-
> mies of civil and religious liberty for ages, is enabled by its
> experience to penetrate into its dark designs—to detect its
> duplicity—to determine on which side of the question it stands
> —has on account of such things been persecuted, more than
> any other system of religion whatever—but never been a per-
> secutor, notwithstanding all the endeavors of its enemies to
> prove it.[59]

With such a spirit prevalent in a rapidly growing
part of the community, there was inevitably a revolt
against one of New England's peculiar institutions, a
church supported by taxation. At the beginning of the
period under discussion such a system existed in all the
states except Rhode Island. The latter state lacks this
phase of the Republican movement.

The privileged position of the clergy, unlike that of
the lawyers and propertied classes whose ascendency
was due to local conditions or their own exertions, was
vulnerable. It was open to attack by legislation. It
was merely a question of time until the potential energy

---

[59] The Age of Inquiry; or Reason and Revelation in Harmony with
Each Other; operating against all Tyranny and Infidelity: intended as
a clue to the present political controversy in the United States. By A
True Baptist. Hartford, 1804, 12. See also 15, 25.

created by the growing hostility to the clergy and the accessions to the minor denominations should be converted into an attempt to destroy the Establishments. In Connecticut, local conditions required a more drastic remedy and led to the Republican attempts to abolish the old charter government and substitute a modern constitution.[60] In 1818 this effort was finally successful.

The laws regarding taxation for religious purposes were not severe. By the Massachusetts constitution of 1780 it was provided that towns should be authorized to make provision for the institution of public worship, and for "the support and maintenance of public Protestant teachers of piety, religion, and morality." In case a member objected, his tax could be diverted to the support of the teacher of his own denomination, otherwise the money was to be paid to the support of the teacher of the parish or precinct wherein it was raised.[61] In Connecticut dissenters were exempted from taxation in support of the state church on presentation of certificates of membership, but all persons were still taxed for religious purposes.[62] A similar system prevailed in New Hampshire and Vermont.[63] While the actual oppression of this system was not great, there were constant opportunities for petty annoyances and it still constituted a form of union between church and state. "To most of you who live in New England, I know what your difficulties are," writes A True Baptist. "The fetters of the state religion were put upon you in your infancy, when you could not help yourselves, either by word or deed: and during your minority, you were par-

[60] This phase of the Republican movement in New England has received an excellent treatment by Greene, Religious Liberty in Conn., 369-496. This should be read in connection with this chapter.

[61] Lauer, Church and State in New England, 84.

[62] *Ibid.*, 89.

[63] *Ibid.*, 89-90.

tially holden by it in your fathers' names. . . . And
lest after all you should hobble away, the political
fetters were clapt on at twenty one; and thus fettered
on both sides you can go neither backwards nor for-
wards from that religion; but must support it according
to law, unless you have a grant from the law makers.
And now your priests and politicians complain bitterly
of us, for attempting to break these fetters; they are
afraid if you get them off of one side, you will soon
get them off the other.''[64] The breaking up of the religious establishment and of the dominance of one church
was a necessary event in developing a party system.

The movement towards disestablishment was, in general, carried on under Republican auspices, although
there were probably many Federalists who had little
sympathy for the existing system.[65] In Connecticut,
two of the most prominent Republican leaders, Kirby
and Granger, had come forward as opponents of a
scheme to appropriate the returns from sales of state
land in the west for the use of churches and schools.[66]
Both had attacked the proposal as an injustice to a
large minority of citizens, and incompatible with republican institutions.[67] At the same time, Timothy Dwight,
by a famous sermon on the same topic, took his place
as the leading champion of the regular order.[68]
Another interesting figure in this movement was John
Leland, a Baptist clergyman who had taken part in the

[64] The Age of Inquiry, 25. *Ibid.*, 15. To Federalists, ''The first principles of your cause, in my opinion, as I have before noted, are the same
which lie at the foundation of all tyrannical religions and governments,
at the foundation of all church and state combinations.''

[65] GREENE, Religious Liberty in Conn., 376-377.

[66] For a discussion of this bill, *ibid.*, 381-392.

[67] The debate in the legislature was published in Am. Mercury, May 16,
1794.

[68] This sermon appears in Conn. Courant, March 16, 23, 30, 1795.

Virginia disestablishment. He afterwards removed to Connecticut and later to Cheshire, in Berkshire County, Mass. He was an enthusiastic admirer of Jefferson and an apostle of Republicanism.[69] His opinions on an elective judiciary have already been quoted. Another Baptist, Elias Smith of Portsmouth, was at once a foe of the Establishment and an advocate of Republicanism.[70] In 1808 he founded a religious publication, *The Herald of Gospel Liberty,* in which he attacked the clergy and upheld the Republican party with equal zeal.[71] In an early number he writes: "There are people in the country who still desire a religion supported by the government. . . . These people have remained among us like the seven nations in Canaan to be overcome by little and little, and when we as a nation have been inattentive to our privileges, they have been as briars in our eyes, and thorns in our sides. . . . The republican principle is constantly prevailing, and as this prevails religious liberty extends with it." The

[69] See GREENE, Religious Liberty in Conn., 376, 387. Also 541 for a list of his pamphlets on religious liberty. See also F. F. PETITCLERC, Recollections of John Leland. Publications of Berkshire Historical Society, I, 269. Also Some Events in the Life of John Leland, written by Himself. Pittsfield, Mass., 1838. Manasseh Cutler who heard him preach before Congress in 1808 when he had presented the President with a cheese from the Berkshire Republicans, describes him as "the cheesemonger, a poor, ignorant, illiterate, clownish preacher."

[70] See The Life, Conversion, Preaching, Travels and Sufferings of Elias Smith. Written by Himself, Portsmouth, N. H., 1816.

[71] There is an incomplete file of this publication for 1808-1809 in the Boston Public Library.

His opinion of Jefferson is worth quoting. "Jefferson's name will always be held in high esteem by those who love liberty, equality, unity, and peace. . . . I do not think there ever was a chief magistrate so well qualified as he is. His ideas of government and religion accord with the laws of the King of Kings. . . . For this he is hated by hypocrites and those who wish to stamp the people into dust and ashes, in order to acquire ease, wealth, riches, and everlasting reputation, by depriving the people of their rights." January 19, 1809.

dissenters looked to Jefferson as the great leader of their cause and occasional complimentary addresses express their loyalty.[72]

Such men as Leland and Smith were agitators, but the actual work of repealing the public worship laws seems to have been carried out quietly. Vermont was the first state to bring about the reform. In 1801 there was a partial repeal, and in 1807, under the lead of two Baptist and Republican members of the legislature, all previous statutes were repealed.[73] Repeal in New Hampshire was slower in coming. The state boasted that it had fewer aristocratic principles of government and less bigotry in religion than Massachusetts.[74] In 1805 and 1807 laws were passed relieving Universalists and Baptists.[75] Even Smith admitted that "law religion" in this state was less offensive than in Massachusetts and Connecticut.[76] Complete religious liberty came with the passage of the Toleration Act of 1819.

In Connecticut and Massachusetts the feeling against the Establishment steadily grew. In the former state

[72] See Am. Mercury, January 28, 1802. Address of Danbury Baptist Association. *Ibid.*, March 30, 1809. Address of New Lebanon Methodists.

[73] BURRAGE, History of the Baptists, 131. There had been great opposition to the system at an earlier date. See Spooner's Vt. Journal, August 18, October 20, November 3, 10, December 8, 1794. There was also resentment at the activity of the Connecticut and Massachusetts missionaries who were "zealous against Methodists, Baptists, and Universalists." *Ibid.*, February 23, 1795. Conn. Courant, July 28, 1794. See also A Short History of late Ecclesiastical Oppressions in New England and Vermont. By a citizen. Richmond, 1799. This latter has an interesting account of the forfeiture of the Episcopalian glebes by the Vermont legislature.

[74] N. H. Patriot, February 7, 1813.

[75] LAUER, Church and State in New England, 101.

[76] A Discourse on Government and Religion, 40. Also The loving Kindness of God displayed in the Triumph of Republicanism in America; being a Discourse delivered at Taunton, Mass., July 4, 1809, 30. "Civil and religious liberty has triumphed in every part of the union except Connecticut and Massachusetts and a few desolate spots in New Hampshire."

almost the whole political struggle of the early years of the century hinged on the question of religious liberty. While the dissenters were numerous and active the Federalists had the support of the strong Episcopalian body, and until they had alienated that support were able to hold their ground.[77] The adoption of the new constitution of 1818 ended the legal control of the Congregational church in that state. In Massachusetts in the winter of 1807-1808, when the Republicans were for the first time in full control of the state government a Public Worship bill was introduced.[78] Bentley writes that the vote by which it was negatived, 127 to 102, was a fair indication of the relative progress of opinion on the subject. He considered that the rapid increase of the sects would make the passage of such a law inevitable within a few years.[79]

The defeat of the Republicans in this year gave the Federalists control until 1810. In 1811 interest in the subject was renewed by a judicial decision that money received by ministerial taxes could be diverted only to societies regularly incorporated by law.[80] Large numbers of dissenting societies were little more than informal gatherings, and the Federalists in the legislature had more than once shown unwillingness to grant

[77] GREENE, Religious Liberty in Conn., 405, 417, 441-444. The Episcopalians were wealthy and probably of the same social class as the Congregationalists. Ibid., 405. Cf. Dwight's complimentary reference to Episcopal ministers. Travels, I, 177.

[78] House Journal, XXVII, 63.

[79] Diary, III, 345. Ibid., 505. After discussing the extravagances of the Baptists, ''The opposition take hold of this as a plea for an establishment & scruple not to say that the best religion cannot find support in civil society unless it be administered in the same manner, as the Laws support all other concerns which relate to the common safety.''

[80] The decision was printed as a pamphlet. At the Supreme Judicial Court, May term, 1810, in Cumberland, Thomas Barns vs. The Inhabitants of the First Parish in Falmouth. Am. Ant. Soc. Library.

incorporation.[81]   There was a renewed demand for
reform.[82]   In June, 1811, a law was passed exempting
from ministerial taxation all persons producing a cer-
tificate of membership in any other religious society,
incorporate or otherwise.[83]   Complete separation of
church and state did not occur until 1833.

It is difficult to prove whether these public worship
bills were adopted by strict party voting, but there is
no question but that the Republican party held itself
responsible for them and that the Federalists were
strongly opposed to their passage.   An address to the
people of Maine in 1811 reminds them that the Republicans stand for religious liberty while the Federalists
"are friendly to one class of religious worshippers and
promote their interests exclusively."[84]   A similar appeal
to the Massachusetts voters a year later warns them
that the "aristocratic hierarchy" are the enemies of
religious freedom and urges them to keep the government in the hands of the Republicans.[85]

While the Federalist clergy were unsparing in denouncing these opponents, there is little evidence that
the Republicans made religious grounds a basis of personal attack.   In 1812, it is true, Strong and Phillips,
the Federalist candidates for governor and lieutenant-
governor, are held up as "both members of that denomination which has taxed the minor denominations to pay

81 E. Argus, May 2, 1811.   "The Federalists supported the Judiciary
against the Baptists, Methodists, and Sectarians generally.   In one branch
every federal vote was repeatedly given against incorporating those societies with the privilege of admitting members."

82 A considerable number of petitions on this matter are preserved in
Mass. Archives.

83 LAUER, Church and State in New England, 104.   General Laws, 276.
1811, Chap. VI.

84 E. Argus, May 2, 1811.

85 Ind. Chronicle, March 17, 1812.   See also March 23, April 2.

their minister.''[86]   A similar attack on Lieutenant-Governor Cobb appears in 1810.[87]

This phase of Republican activity has considerable significance. Like the movements discussed in the previous chapter it denoted a laudable opposition to a class which had usurped more than a fair share of influence in the community, an influence which was too much on the side of provincialism and conservatism. Its outcome was the complete and final separation of church and state, one of the distinctive features of American polity.

[86] *Ibid.*, March 12, 1812.

[87] E. Argus, March 22, 27, 1810. In latter number appears the following doggerel, in regard to Cobb's alleged intolerance.

> O, had your Honor chanced to live
>   In good Queen Mary's days,
> What hecatombs your zeal would give
>   To Smithfield's hallowed blaze.
>
> Yet modern times may learn from you
>   The blessings of her reign,
> When Fire and Faggots shall subdue
>   The Democrats of Maine.

CHAPTER VIII

THE NATIONAL SIGNIFICANCE OF NEW ENGLAND REPUBLICANISM

The political movement whose growth and activity have been discussed had an importance not confined to New England. The Republican party was a national organization, a fact doubly important since in 1800 its rival had been almost annihilated outside of the New England stronghold. Federalism was still supreme in the latter region at the opening of the century. In view of the attitude which its leaders assumed towards the national government after 1801, the growth of the Republican party was of vital importance to the whole country. The process of creating a nation was still in its early stages; the country was only twelve years away from the state jealousies and disorders of the Confederation. New England was in many ways a distinct region; the character of the people, its institutions, its economic interests, all combined to make it the seat of provincialism. "The people of New England must be conciliated and persuaded," writes Granger to Jefferson early in his first term and advising moderation in removal of Federalist officeholders. "They are all natives whose ancestors long since resided here. They have a kind of national Character—feel all that pride and love of Country—that is—of New England which in old countries have produced such astonishing effects."[1] Should there be a large enough majority of

[1] July 6, 1801. Jefferson Papers, 2d Series, XXXVI, No. 30.

the people arrayed against the national administration, the consequences to national development would be serious.

Although the Republican party lacked a program in the modern sense, although its principles were largely generalities, yet on one question it took an emphatic and definite position. Between 1800 and 1815 it was essentially the party of union and nationalism. Although the Federalist legislature of Massachusetts had declared in 1799 in reply to the Virginia and Kentucky Resolutions that "the several United States are connected by a common interest which ought to render their union indissoluble and that this state will always co-operate with its confederate states in rendering that union productive of mutual security, freedom, and happiness,"[2] the party attitude changed completely with the events of 1800.

During Jefferson's first administration the Federalist press made persistent efforts to arouse ill feeling towards Virginia and the South.[3] "Virginia influence" was as vicious as "French influence." The New England Republican was taunted with being a servant or ally of the South. The measures of the administration were hostile to New England interests, the latter charge becoming still more bitter as foreign complications brought on the restrictive system. An appeal on behalf of the Federalist congressional ticket in Maine in 1802 urges the support of "all those who are not willing to prostrate our national glory at the feet of a Virginia faction."[4] Says an address to the New Hampshire

[2] Senate Journal, XIX, 225.

[3] Am. Mercury. May 20, 1802, accounts for the slow growth of Republicanism in Massachusetts thus, "There is much state pride in Massachusetts and federalism has been kept from sinking there by raising jealousies against Virginia."

[4] Quoted from Portland Gazette by Portsmouth Oracle, October 12, 1802.

farmers, after reminding them of the removal of the stamp tax, the excise on whiskey, and the carriage tax: "Is abolishing these taxes restoring to the mouth of labor the bread it has earned? Is it not suffering the Virginia Nabobs to ride at ease in their carriages?"[5] An appeal on behalf of the Federalist candidate in the York district of Maine states: "Mr. Lord is no Virginian—he is in principle as well as fact a New England man, plain in his manners, sound in his morality, and virtuous in his politics."[6] This is the prevailing tone of the Federalists, their virulence increasing every year until after the war.

The Republican spirit is in marked contrast to that exhibited in the above quotations. "Union is essential to our happiness," reads an appeal on behalf of John Langdon in 1803.[7] "The Federalists are using every base means to dissolve our union. . . . Be on your guard against them."[8] All Republicans must support the Union, its interests are indissoluble. "If one member of the body receives a wound, the whole must feel it."[9] The Federalist disaffection rose in 1804 to the point of conspiracy against the Union.[10] The acquisition of Louisiana was considered a blow at New England inter-

5 Portsmouth Oracle, February 27, 1802. Cf. Conn. Courant, March 23, 1803. "The Pennsylvania Irishmen and Virginians drink whiskey duty free, the southern nabobs ride in untaxed carriages and give notes without paying for the stamp. The poor pay the same duties on brown sugar, salt, coffee, bohea tea, and molasses."

Cf. Col. Centinel, April 20, 1803, in reference to the recent election in Connecticut. "The satellites of Old Dominion owe their mortification to the exertions and steady habits of the owners and cultivators of the soil."

6 Portsmouth Oracle, October 26, 1802.

7 N. H. Gazette, January 25, 1803.

8 Ibid., February 1.

9 Ibid., February 15.

10 For a discussion of this movement see Adams U. S., II, 166-191.

ests,[11] and the Republicans were well aware of the dangerous situation in this year. There are savage denunciations of "the demagogues who still threaten a dissolution of the Union."[12] Republicans must "repel as well as reprobate all attempts and measures that naturally tend to a dissolution of the union and use every possible exertion to make the state government harmonize with the national."[13] An appeal to the New Hampshire voters reads, "to preserve our glorious union a wise choice of representatives to Congress is of momentous importance."[14] "You may guard the safety, or seal the death warrant of the national union," says an address to the voters of Worcester County, Mass.[15] It was in this year that the Massachusetts legislature proposed an amendment to the United States constitution abolishing the "three fifths" clause and basing representation on free white population. This was rejected by most of the states, greatly to the satisfaction of the Republicans.[16] The sweeping victory

[11] The following is a typical utterance. Portsmouth Oracle, October 13, 1804. "New England, the seat of commerce, of industry, of wealth and active strength is gradually losing her relative weight in the general delegation. Her ancient rights like morning clouds are passing beyond the mountains to fall in prolific showers upon the territories of Ohio, of Indiana, of Mississippi, of Louisiana and the Pacific Ocean."

[12] Ind. Chronicle, April 9, 1804. Also N. H. Gazette, April 24. The Nat'l Aegis, May 30, denounces. "This insidious, this inflammatory, this treasonable attempt to raise jealousies between the different divisions of the country."

[13] N. H. Gazette, February 14, 1804.

[14] Ibid., August 14.

[15] Nat'l Aegis, October 31, 1804. The same spirit is found in an oration by Joseph Chandler at Monmouth, Me. E. Argus, September 6. The Republican toasts at Fourth of July and other gatherings during this year give "the Union of the States" a prominent place.

[16] The Col. Centinel, November 17, 1804, states that Rhode Island, "that little satellite of Virginia," and Vermont having rejected this amendment would doubtless "receive a 'well done' from Virginia."

of the party at the November election was taken as a decisive rebuke to the Federalist designs. "It demonstrates the unity of the American people on the cardinal points of their political concerns. It proves that, however from the influence of momentary prejudice or ignorance they may differ for a day, they become when well informed, one homogeneous and solid mass. Let us not hereafter be told that the several states are composed of such discordant materials as to be incapable of harmonious action. Let us not be told that the feelings, the principles, and the views of one section are hostile to those of another. . . . This early triumph of principle is eminently owing to leading causes; the attempts recently made to dismember the empire, and those made to enlist the passions and prejudices of the East against the South."[17]

The disloyal conduct of the Federalists while the embargo was in force is well known. The effect of this measure on the political strength of the Republican party was serious, but there was still a large body in most states only a few hundred short of a majority, which stood loyally by the government. This minority recognized the dangers of the situation. The resolutions of the Bristol County Republicans denounce the "powerful combination of persons" at Boston who "have sought to organize a system of distrust and opposition which should paralyze the national government and break asunder the unity of the states" and pledge the party support for the Union.[18] In the Connecticut legislature the Republican minority condemned

[17] Ind. Chronicle, December 13, 1804.

[18] *Ibid.*, October 10, 1808. Almost every number of this paper from August, 1808, to March, 1809, contains reports of loyal meetings.

On June 8, 1809, it is declared, "Federalism is another term for hostility to the Union."

the conduct of the governor in refusing the Secretary of War the use of militia to enforce the embargo.[19] Their example was followed by Republicans in many towns who signed resolutions pledging support to the national government.[20] Republican feeling in Rhode Island was similar.[21]

The seven years following the laying of the embargo were full of hardship for New England. Commercial restrictions were followed by war; the hostility of the Federalists kept rising steadily. The victory of Elbridge Gerry in 1810 was announced as "a victory for the friends of Union."[22] Gerry in his various messages was careful to emphasize the need of loyalty to the Union and even went so far as to justify a removal from office during the latter part of his administration because the incumbent was "trying to subvert the national Government and to sever the union of the states."[23]

The party held to the same principles throughout the war. Not long after the outbreak of hostilities a convention of Hampshire County Republicans declared,

[19] Conn. Courant, March 8, 1809. Am. Mercury, March 2.

[20] Am. Mercury, March 10, 17, 23, 30, April 6, 13, 1809.

[21] R. I. Republican, April 12, 18, 1809. The latter number states in regard to the conduct of the legislature: "What is this but unqualified and open Rebellion? . . . If New England break from the union we are crushed between Massachusetts and Connecticut and will probably be divided between them. . . . The Boston junto have dictated to their understrapping junto of Rhode Island."

The following anecdote appearing in a number of Republican papers illustrates the feeling of the day. A "prominent Federalist" on his way to Washington speaks of the dissolution of the Union, and asks "In case New Englanders should rise, would the New Jersey militia act against them?" A Republican replies, "I trust, sir, there are now, as there were in '76, whigs enough in New England to keep the tories down." Ind. Chronicle, December 19, 1808.

[22] Ind. Chronicle, April 9.

[23] Col. Centinel, February 19, 1812.

"Should the leaders of the Federalist party call a state or New England convention according to their contemplated plan we solemnly declare that we shall regard such an act as a preparatory step on the part of our domestic enemies to organize a force for the destruction of everything dear to us, and that we shall take such decisive measures as so alarming a crisis will imperiously demand."[24] This was the tone of the party two years later when Massachusetts issued the call for the Hartford Convention. Several notable speeches were delivered by Republican members of the legislature, all denouncing the proposed convention as "treason and rebellion." The Maine members were especially active in opposition to the secession projects of the Federalists.[25] In Rhode Island the minority conducted a determined opposition to sending delegates, and after defeat adopted a series of resolutions declaring that "the proposed convention bears the garb and complexion of sedition, insurrection, rebellion and treason."[26]

The history of the Hartford Convention need not be discussed here. It should not be forgotten that it did not represent the unanimous sentiment of New England. In Vermont and New Hampshire parties were evenly matched and neither state was officially represented. In Maine the Republicans were actually in the majority. In the previous February the *American Mercury* in discussing the threats of the Federalists, remarked: "They will resolve and remonstrate with terrible fury. . . .

[24] Ind. Chronicle, July 27, 1812. See also July 15, 18.

[25] See speeches of Albion K. Parris, E. Argus, June 16, July 7, October 27; of M. L. Hill, July 21; Timothy Fuller, March 3; J. Holmes, June 30, July 7, 1814.

[26] R. I. Republican, November 9, 16, 23, gives a summary of proceedings of legislature and much interesting comment.

See also Am. Mercury, November 8, 15, 22, December 13, 27, for Connecticut opinions.

The wisest of the faction know the extent of their power and confine their aims to possibilities. . . . The national government can rely on the support and co-operation of 100,000 Republicans in New England. Perhaps we do not feel as much alarmed as we ought. Be well prepared for every exigency."[27]

Enough has been quoted to show that the Republican party always maintained the principle of loyalty to the Union. Whether this would have been sufficient to have led to civil war had the Federalists actually seceded, it is impossible to say. Had the party been as small a minority as in 1798, New England would have had few ties with the rest of the country. The presence of a well-organized party, never more than a few thousand votes in the minority, preaching loyalty and nationalism throughout the fourteen years when the opposing party was steadily tending in the opposite direction, was an important factor in national life.

The Republican party was essentially American. Kendall remarked that "the anti-federalists in politics are all optimists in philosophy; and everything in the United States (federalism excepted) is the best of all possible things."[28] They helped to make New England like the rest of the country. The introduction of "the detestable practice of electioneering" might have evil features, but it helped make American parties and politics uniform from Maine to Georgia. The breaking

[27] February 15, 1814.

[28] Travels, II, 233. The occasion of his remark was an argument between the innkeeper and the clergyman of Dighton, Mass. "Every person in the United States," said my landlord, "is happy: not one in ten thousand is unhappy." "You, you are all unhappy," replied his reverend opponent: "not one in ten thousand is happy: you carry fire-brands in your bosom; you all want to be kings!" The Salem Register, January 18, 1802, attacks the Federalist practice of "belittling everything American."

down of the rule of family, clerical and legal alliances was part of the same process. The country was expanding; New England could not forever have the same influence in the nation, and it was wasted energy for the Federalists to rail against Kentucky or Louisiana. Perhaps the essential difference in the two parties appears in two toasts, both to "the Union of the States." The Federalist, "Wo to them who vote down the Wall of Partition, and let in the prairie dogs and wolves of the wilderness, to snarl at and devour our children."[29] The Republican, "Oceans the boundary, eternity the duration, and infamy to those who advise their dissolution."[30]

30 E. Argus, June 14, 1804.
29 Col. Centinel, July 7, 1813.

CHAPTER IX

PARTY DISTRIBUTION

A. *Distribution of Parties, 1811.* Dotted areas, Federalist; shaded, Republican. Based on vote for governor except in Connecticut, returns in Massachusetts Archives and as published for respective states in *New Hampshire Gazette, Vermont Republican, Rhode Island Republican.* The distribution in Connecticut is based on incomplete returns of the vote for governor published in *Connecticut Mirror,* and representation in Assembly as indicated by vote on resolution condemning Non-Intercourse. Yeas and nays on this resolution were published in *Connecticut Courant,* June 5, with comment that all voting against resolutions were Democrats.

B. *Vote on Religious Liberty Bills.* For religious liberty, shaded; against, dotted. A few Connecticut towns with evenly divided vote indicated by parallel lines. These bills deal with the question of supporting the clergy by public taxation. Those in Vermont and New Hampshire abolished this practice, the Baptist petition in Connecticut was a request for such action. The Massachusetts bill allowed exemption on presentation of properly signed certificates.

1. Vermont. "An act to repeal a certain act and parts of an act therein mentioned relating to the support of the Gospel." Assembly Journal, session of 1807, 118. (October 20.) Yeas, 105; nays, 71.

2. New Hampshire. "An Act in amendment of an act entitled, an act for regulating towns and the choice of town officers, passed February 8, 1791." House Journal, June session, 1819, 286. (June 25.) Yeas, 95; nays, 88.

3. Massachusetts. "Will the House reconsider their vote

passed this day whereby they decided that the Bill entitled 'An Act respecting Public Worship and Religious Freedom' should pass to be engrossed.'' House Journal, XXXII, 94. Yeas and nays, Appendix III.

4. Connecticut. Vote on accepting the report of committee to which was referred Baptist petition. Yeas and nays published in *Connecticut Courant*, June 1, 1803.

C. Massachusetts. Federal, dotted; Republican, shaded. Based on vote for governor, returns in Mass. Archives.

D. District of Maine, same elections.

1. Election of 1797.
2. Election of 1802.
3. Election of 1807.

An examination of the accompanying maps reveals some interesting facts in regard to the distribution of the parties. In Massachusetts the election of 1797, one of the first regular party tests, shows the parties in force in certain areas which they continue to hold in after years. In 1802 and 1807 (Maps 2, 3) these areas are seen to have spread somewhat so that they constitute continuous party zones. Only the District of Maine shows any remarkable transformation, the causes of which have already been explained. In Massachusetts proper, Federalism is found at its greatest strength in a strip of varying width along the coast and in the great interior area of Hampshire and Worcester counties, Republicanism being in control of the intervening area and of Berkshire in the west. In New Hampshire the Federalists were strong in the western counties of the Connecticut Valley and along the lower Merrimac, while the Republicans occupied the great interior area of the state. In Rhode Island, the Republicans usually controlled the interior towns, Federalism being found at its greatest strength in Providence and along the seacoast.

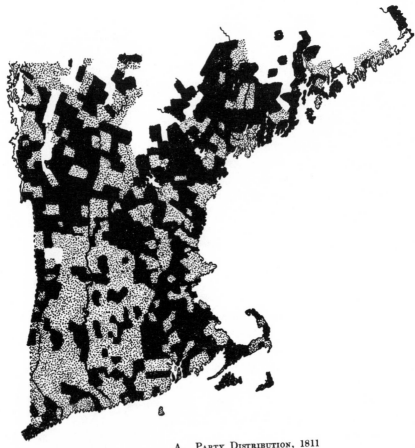

A. Party Distribution, 1811

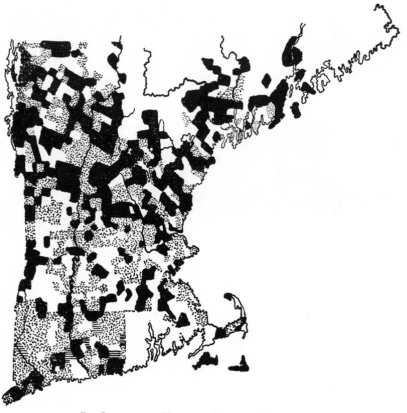

B. Legislative Votes on Religious Liberty

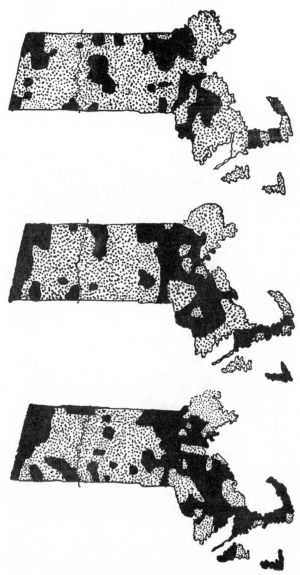

C. PARTY DISTRIBUTION, MASSACHUSETTS
1797, 1802, 1807

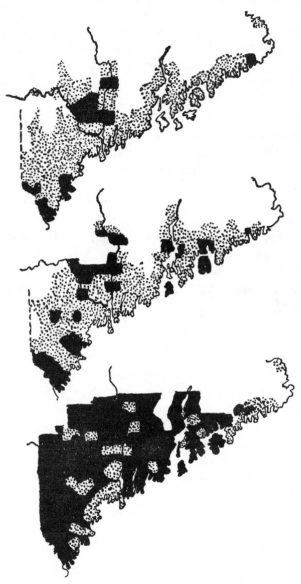

D. PARTY DISTRIBUTION, DISTRICT OF MAINE
1797, 1802, 1807

Looking at New England as a whole the party grouping becomes still clearer. The coast towns, as has been already remarked, were for the most part devoted to commercial interests, which were strongly opposed to the policy of the Republicans. The Lake Champlain region of Vermont with its extensive commerce with Canada also shows strong Federalist tendencies. In Maine the same fact is apparent, the coast towns being in marked contrast to the overwhelmingly Republican character of the interior. Kendall, who visited the district in 1807, found that the region around the lower Kennebec and Androscoggin, which was devoted to commerce and ship building was opposed to the Republican advocacy of war with England.[1]

There was, it is true, considerable Republican strength along the coast, and in the earlier years of the movement the Federalists had remarked that it was in the seaports that "Jacobinism and yellow fever were endemical."[2] Fisher Ames' remark in regard to the spread of Jacobinism from the "docks and mob" to the rural population (1799) has already been quoted. Nantucket and Cape Cod always show Republican tendencies, as do Portsmouth, Salem, and Marblehead. The outrages of England on American shipping and the fondness of the Federalists for that country would probably not be agreeable to the seamen even if ship owners were willing to endure them in view of the profits of commerce.

The most striking feature of the political map of New England is the region of the Connecticut River, "whose stream like the Nile in Egypt fertilizes its banks from its source to the ocean and causes them to produce abundant harvests of Federalism and unwavering

---

[1] Travels, III, 142.
[2] Col. Centinel, March 10, 1801. See also June 14, 1797; March 24, 1802.

attachment to right principles.''³ In Vermont, always
a state with strong Republican tendencies, the division
of sentiment is plain, Federalism flourishing along the
river. In 1798 Matthew Lyon noted the fact and blamed
this part of the state for the intolerant measures of the
legislature. ''The east has always been considered as
the source of light and knowledge, but taking a confined
view, circumscribed by the bounds of this state we find
that source contaminated with falsehood, darkness,
ignorance and stupidity.''⁴ A glance at Map B shows
that this region stood out against the demand for religious freedom. It also supported the Hartford Convention, Windham County, Vermont, and Grafton and
Cheshire, New Hampshire, sending delegates, while in
the Massachusetts legislature the vote of the representatives of the river counties was overwhelmingly in favor
of the convention.⁵

The valley was a distinct area. Timothy Dwight, to
whom the region was the most beautiful and ''respectable'' in New England, noted that its inhabitants possessed a similarity in character throughout its whole
length. Settlement had moved north and most of the
inhabitants of the valley were also natives. Churches,
schools and books were abundant, the people were industrious and poverty unknown.⁶ ''Steadiness of character, softness of manners, a disposition to read, respect
for the laws and magistrates, a strong sense of liberty,
blended with an equally strong sense of the indispen-
sable importance of energetic government, are all

---

³ Col. Centinel, March 11, 1801.
⁴ The Scourge of Aristocracy. Castleton, 1798, 96. (In library of Yale
University.)
⁵ Hampden, 12-3; Hampshire, 19-0; Franklin, 20-2. House Journal,
XXXV. Appendix, 2d Session.
⁶ Travels, II, 333-338 *passim*.

extensively predominant in this region.'"[7] Contemporary Republican opinion ascribed its Federalism to the conservative character of the inhabitants and the influence over them of the clergy and magistrates. A writer in 1801 explains the matter by stating that a few leaders from Boston by joining the remnants of the old Tory party had swayed public opinion for many years and persuaded the people that the agricultural prosperity following the outbreak of war in Europe was due to their own policy.[8]

A similar opinion appears in New Hampshire. Referring to the large Federal towns on the Connecticut River: "We believe the mass of the people in these towns to be honest and well disposed; but the influence of a few designing men, federal lawyers, shopkeepers and clergymen upon them is astonishing. It is sufficient for these duped people that certain 'larned men' have told them our rulers are under French influence and infidels and knaves without inquiring further to ascertain the real facts.'"[9] It is natural that Republicanism with its independence of thought, its contempt for tradition and clerical authority, should make little headway among such people as compared with other areas.

Examination of Map A brings out very clearly the strength of Republicanism extending in an irregular belt across northern New England, broken here and there by Federalist areas, noticeably by the Connecticut Valley. The Green Mountain territory in Vermont—the Berkshires in Massachusetts form a continuation of the

---

[7] *Ibid.*, 334.

[8] Ind. Chronicle, February 5, 1801. See also May 4, September 24.

[9] N. H. Patriot, March 22, 1814. Cf. AMES, Diary, January 31, 1804. "It is amazing to consider the delusion under which the people about Conn. river remain as to politics by means of aristocratic papers and preaching. Mrs. Wetherby returned from Northampton says they still curse Jefferson tho' he has denied himself the powers put in his hands,'' etc.

same area—northern and central New Hampshire, and the interior of Maine were largely Republican. These were the newer regions of New England, settled largely since the close of the French and Indian War, and still more rapidly since 1783. The influences which contributed to the political solidarity of the valley were here lacking.[10] The important influence of Congregationalism was less than in the old settlements, and as has been shown, it was among the new settlements that the Baptists and Methodists made such gains. The settlers were naturally men of less property and greater individuality, "the sons of resolution, enterprise and industry," whose only luxuries were "the budding hopes of better times and kinder moments," as one writer describes the settlers of Maine.[11] Dwight, in a well-known passage occasioned by a journey through Vermont, has left a Federalist impression of the character of the settlers, "usually such as have met with difficulty at home," "the discontented, the enterprising, the ambitious and the covetous."[12] The doctrines of Thomas Jefferson were the natural opinions of the outlying settlements.

[10] Cf. the following comment on the early progress of the Republican party, quoted from Nat'l Intelligencer by Ind. Chronicle, November 15, 1802. "To these events a spirit of resistance, calm, deliberate, energetic, gradually arose which infused its efficacious influence through the whole extent of the union. From the center it passed to the borders of the empire where it acquired additional strength. Remote from scenes of mercenary traffic, it found among the independent yeomanry minds unprejudiced by foreign attachment, minds truly American, minds which for the most part had unfolded since the era of independence. The honest exercise of an independent and well informed judgment always leads to truth and it has been the fortunate lot of our western brethren never to disregard or disobey it. The western states have always been republican. . . . It is to these states we owe much of our political happiness."

[11] E. Argus, January 18, 1810.

[12] Travels, II, 458.

A comparison of the areas occupied by the Republicans and those of the Anti-federalists of 1788 shows an interesting resemblance. (See map in Libby, Geographical Distribution of Vote on Federal Constitution.) The Anti-federalist region of central New Hampshire—an area which Dwight describes as having little connection with either the western or eastern counties—is in 1811 the stronghold of Republicanism in that state. In Massachusetts the old Anti-federalist area shows a considerable shrinkage, due probably to the emigration of the discontented in the years following the Shays Rebellion and the adoption of the Constitution.[13] York County and the interior settlements of Maine were also Anti-federalist and became Republican. Rhode Island shows the old division, the interior parts of the state Anti-federalist and Republican, the commercial regions Federalist. In Connecticut, Federalism was so predominant as to furnish little of interest in regard to distribution. It is curious to note that as in 1788, West Springfield, Mass., and Suffield, Conn., with a few adjoining towns form a Republican island in the Federalist stream of the Connecticut Valley.

As has been already remarked, New England was a region of uniform character. The population was almost entirely from the same source; except for the commercial and agricultural there were few, if any, great varieties of economic interest, facts which render a complete explanation of political conditions practically impossible. This explanation may be sought in the character of local influences, leadership, and tradition and the above is a suggestion as to the more important of them.

13 MORSE, Fed. Party in Mass., 183, 184.

BIBLIOGRAPHICAL NOTES

BIBLIOGRAPHY

I. The present study has been based very largely on the newspapers of the period. The following have been used.

Abbreviations

A. A. S.—American Antiquarian Society.
B. A.—Boston Athenæum.
Y. U.—Yale University.
B. P. L.—Boston Public Library.
R. I. H. S.—Rhode Island Historical Society.

New Hampshire:

Dartmouth Gazette, Hanover, Fed.
    B. P. L. has file 1807-1811, 1813.
New Hampshire Gazette, Portsmouth, Rep.
    B. A. has excellent file of this paper almost complete
    1800-1815. The leading party organ in the state.
New Hampshire Patriot, Concord, Rep.
    A. A. S. file covers period 1809-1815, many deficiencies. Particularly good for war period.
Oracle of the Day, Portsmouth (after 1803, Portsmouth Oracle), Fed.
    Y. U. file covers 1796-1800, 1801-1809.
Political Observatory, Walpole, Rep.
    A. A. S. has file 1803-1804.

Vermont:

Spooner's Vermont Journal, Windsor, Rep.
    A. A. S. has incomplete files covering the period. Is
    a valuable source of information for Vermont affairs.
Freeman's Press, Montpelier, Fed.
    B. P. L. file 1809-1811.
Vermont Republican, Windsor.
    A. A. S. file covers 1809-1815.

Massachusetts:

Boston Patriot, Rep.

B. P. L. file complete, 1809-1815.

Columbian Centinel, Boston, Fed.

B. P. L. file complete, 1790-1815.   One of the best sources for New England political history at this time.   Has considerable information on matters outside of Massachusetts.

Eastern Argus, Portland, Rep.

B. A. file complete, 1803-1811. B. P. L., 1812-1814. Has a great deal of valuable information on District of Maine.

Independent Chronicle and Universal Advertiser, Boston, Rep.

B. P. L. files complete, 1790-1815.   The most important Republican paper in New England.

Massachusetts Spy, Worcester, Fed.

B. P. L. has almost complete file for entire period. An ably edited paper with good quotations from contemporaries.

National Aegis, Worcester, Rep.

B. P. L. file 1801-1815.

New England Palladium, Boston, Fed.

B. A. has excellent file, 1801-1815.

Portland Gazette, Portland, Fed.

B. P. L. file 1806-1807, 1810-1811.

Salem Register, Rep., 1800-1815.

B. P. L. file excellent except for 1806.

Rhode Island:

United States Chronicle, Providence, Fed.

Y. U. file 1788-1797, 1799-1800.

Providence Phœnix, Providence, Rep.

R. I. H. S. file, 1802-1808.

Rhode Island Republican, Newport, Rep.

Y. U. file, 1809-1815.

Connecticut:

Connecticut Courant, Hartford, Fed.
    Y. U. file complete, 1790-1815. A very valuable source
    for New England politics, ranking with Col. Centinel.
American Mercury, Hartford, Rep.
    Y. U. file complete, 1790-1815. One of the best Repub-
    lican papers.

II. Of the legislative journals, only those of Vermont and
New Hampshire have been printed. Those of the other states
are available in manuscript.

The Records of the Council of Safety and Governor and
Council of the State of Vermont. 8 vols. Montpelier, 1873-
1880. Vols. IV-VI cover this period. This is a very useful
publication containing biographical sketches and other material necessary to a study of Vermont politics.

Election returns have been preserved only in Massachusetts,
and in New Hampshire after 1802.

The Massachusetts State Library has, practically complete,
the published acts and resolves of the New England states for
this period.

III. General works on this period have tended to look only
at the larger aspects of party history.

ADAMS, HENRY. History of the United States. 9 vols. New
    York, 1889-1891. Is indispensable for any study of the
    period.

BEARD, C. E. The Economic Origins of Jeffersonian Democracy.
    New York, 1915. The most recent and suggestive contri-
    bution to the subject.

HILDRETH, RICHARD. History of the United States. 6 vols.
    New York, 1849-1856. His treatment of political parties is
    clear and comprehensive, though showing a Federalist bias.

McMASTER, J. B. History of the People of the United States
    from the Revolution to the Civil War. 8 vols. New York,
    1883-1913. Is valuable as showing American habits and
    opinions during the period.

WINSOR, JUSTIN. Narrative and Critical History of America. 8 vols. Boston, 1884-1889. Vol. VII, pp. 267-278, has an interesting sketch of Federalist and Republican parties by Alexander Johnston. Bibliographical notes, 294-330.

Local and state histories are of little value. The following however furnish some useful information:

BARRY, J. S. History of Massachusetts. 3 vols. Boston, 1855-1857. Vol. III deals with Commonwealth period to 1820.

HOLLAND, J. S. History of Western Massachusetts. 2 vols. Springfield, 1855.

HOLLISTER, G. H. History of Connecticut, from the First Settlement of the Colony. 2 vols. Hartford, 1857.

THOMPSON, ZADOCK. History of Vermont, Natural, Civil, and Statistical. Burlington, 1842.

WILLIAMSON, W. D. History of the State of Maine. 2 vols. Hallowell, 1832.

IV. The letters of the period contain little information on local affairs. The great Pickering Collection, in possession of the Massachusetts Historical Society, deals almost entirely with matters of national interest. The Plumer MSS. and Jefferson Papers in the Library of Congress contain some material of value.

ADAMS, H. Documents relating to New England Federalism, 1800-1815. Boston, 1877.

AMES, NATHANIEL. Diary. MSS. in possession of Dedham Historical Society. Extracts published in Dedham Historical Register, I-XIV. Throws considerable light on the opinions of a radical Republican.

AMES, S. Works of Fisher Ames. 2 vols. Boston, 1854. Valuable as illustrating Federalist opinion and containing incidental references to local affairs.

BENTLEY, W. J. Diary. Published by Essex Institute. 4 vols. Salem, 1905-1914. An invaluable source of information on religious, political, and social conditions in New England, 1783-1819.

GIBBS, G. Memoirs of the Administrations of Washington and John Adams. New York, 1846.

JEFFERSON. Writings. Washington ed. 9 vols. New York, 1861. Ford ed. 10 vols. New York, 1892-1899. Jefferson kept a close watch on New England politics and occasionally makes some interesting observations.

LODGE, H. C. The Life and Letters of George Cabot. Boston, 1895.

V. Biographies throw little light on New England Republicanism. The biographies of Timothy Pickering, Jeremiah Smith, Josiah Quincy, Manasseh Cutler, Stephen Higginson and other Federalists pay little or no attention to the opposing party. The recently published Life and Letters of Harrison Gray Otis, by S. E. Morison, Boston, 1913, is a valuable addition to the political history of Federalism of this period. The following are practically the only biographies of New England Republicans.

AMORY, T. C. Life of James Sullivan. 2 vols. Boston, 1859.

AUSTIN, J. T. The Life of Elbridge Gerry. 2 vols. Boston, 1828-1829. The latter part of Gerry's career has been slighted.

McLAUGHLIN, J. F. Matthew Lyon, the Hampden of Congress: a Biography. New York, 1900. The interest is largely personal, and no attention has been paid to the background of Lyon's career.

PLUMER, WILLIAM, JR. Life of William Plumer. Boston, 1857.

STORY, W. W. Life and Letters of Joseph Story. 2 vols. Boston, 1851.

Concise information on most of the characters prominent in politics of this period is given in Appleton's National Cyclopædia of American Biography. 14 vols. New York, 1898-1906. Town and other local histories frequently furnish biographical information.

VI. Interesting descriptive material occurs in the following:

DWIGHT, TIMOTHY. Travels in New England and New York. 4 vols. New Haven, 1821-1822.

KENDALL, EDWARD A. Travels through the Northern Parts of the United States, in the Years 1807 and 1808. 3 vols. New York, 1809.

COFFIN, P. Memoir and Journals. Coll. Me. Hist. Soc., IV.

ROBBINS, T. Diary. Edited by I. N. Tarbox. 2 vols. Boston, 1886-1887. Vol. I covers 1796-1825.

VII. The following have considerable information on religious questions and the growth of dissent.

Asbury's Journal. 3 vols. New York, 1821. An account of missionary labors in New England.

BENEDICT, DAVID. A General History of the Baptist Denomination in America and other parts of the world. Boston, 1813.

BURRAGE, HENRY S. A History of the Baptists in New England. Philadelphia, 1894.

STEVENS, ABEL. Memorials of the Introduction of Methodism into the Eastern States. Boston, 1843.

Memorials of the Early Progress of Methodism in the Eastern States. Boston, 1852.

The Life, Conversion, Preaching, Travels and Sufferings of Elias Smith. Written by himself. Portsmouth, N. H., 1816. The autobiography of a prominent leader in the movement for religious liberty.

No attempt is here made to enumerate sermons. The Massachusetts State Library has a complete file of the election sermons of this period for both Massachusetts and Connecticut.

See MORSE, Federal Party in Massachusetts, 194-205, for list of printed sermons.

VIII. The following special studies are very helpful in their respective fields.

ALLEN, W. Bingham Land. In Collections of Me. Hist. Soc., VII.

DALLINGER, F. W. Nominations for Elective Offices in the United States. New York, 1897.

BATES, F. G. Rhode Island and the Formation of the Union.
New York, 1898.

BEARD, C. A. The Economic Origins of Jeffersonian Democracy.
New York, 1915.

GREENE, M. L. The Development of Religious Liberty in Connecticut. Cambridge, 1905.

HAZEN, C. D. Contemporary American Opinion of the French
Revolution. Johns Hopkins University Studies. Extra
volume XVI. Baltimore, 1897.

LAUER, P. E. Church and State in New England. Johns Hop·
kins University Studies. Baltimore, 1892.

LUETSCHER, S. D. Early Political Machinery in the United
States. Philadelphia, 1903.

LIBBY, O. G. The Geographical Distribution of the Vote of
Thirteen States on the Federal Constitution, 1787-1788.
Madison, Wis., 1894.

MORSE, A. E. The Federalist Party in Massachusetts to the
year 1800. Princeton, 1909.

STANWOOD, E. The Massachusetts Election in 1806. In Proc.
of Mass. Hist. Soc., 2d Series, XX.

The Separation of Maine from Massachusetts. *Ibid.*, 3d Series,
I.

WELLING, J. C. Connecticut Federalism. In Addresses, lectures
and other papers. Cambridge, 1904.

IX. The pamphlet literature of the period is extensive.
The Massachusetts Historical Society, the Boston Atheneum,
and American Antiquarian Society have extensive collections
of pamphlets and broadsides. The Yale University Library
is rich in Connecticut material. The chronological classification
adopted by the American Antiquarian Society for the period
prior to 1820 makes their collection more readily accessible to
the investigator. This class of material is, in general, of the
most ephemeral character, but illustrates phases of public
opinion. Such tracts as have been used in the course of this
study have been given by full title in text or footnotes and are
here omitted.

INDEX

INDEX

Adams, John
  re-elected Vice President, 9
  supported by New England, 13
  administration of, 14
Adams, John Quincy, 60, 83, 117
Adams, Samuel, 12
Agricultural interests, Republican
  support of, 99 ff.
American Mercury
  on Republican progress in Con-
    necticut, 31
  on Jefferson's success in Massa-
    chusetts, 51
  on class rule, 112
  on universal suffrage, 123
  on Federalist disloyalty, 157
Ames, Fisher
  member of first Congress, 1
  contest with Charles Jarvis, 10
  on situation 1798, 24
  on Jacobinism, 32, 36
  on importance of state control, 36
  on the press, 68
  forecast of Jefferson administra-
    tion, 76
  on Federalist Party, 76
  on Democracy, 109
Ames, Nathaniel
  on Massachusetts resolutions, 1798,
    19
  on taxation, 25
  on popular restiveness, 1800, 31
  on committee functions, 65
  distributes party literature, 1800,
    68
  on Democracy, 109
  on lawyers, 114
  on clerical politicians, 134

Anti-federalism
  influence in early Congressional
    elections, 5
  comparison of areas of with Re-
    publican, 168
Aristocracy
  Republican opposition to, 4, 23,
    111 ff.
  Independent Chronicle on, 98
  Abraham Bishop on, 111
  William Bentley on, 127
  clergy and, 138
Austin, Charles, 120

Bacon, John, 23
Banking
  importance of question in New
    Hampshire, 29, 53, 103
  William Plumer on, 53
  Republican hostility to, 102 ff.
Baptists
  Bentley on, 137
  growth in numbers, 136
  strength in frontier settlements,
    137, 140
  Republicanism of, 141, 143 ff.
Bentley, William
  on Jay Treaty, 11
  on hostilities with France, 25
  on electioneering, 1800, 29
  on election of 1808, 83
  on Republican personnel, 106
  on James Sullivan, 117
  on judiciary, 118
  on aristocracy, 127
  on clerical intolerance, 133, 142
  on dissenting sects, 137 ff.
Berkshire County, Massachusetts, 15,
  20, 90, 168